To design anything requires a pattern, including life itself. In every chapter of this book, Judy Couchman gives us that pattern, through real-life examples of women with dedication, creativity, balance, and acceptance.

When we learn to look honestly within and ask questions, life's patterns emerge. Judy's personal experience and insightful words provide us the tools for looking within and asking the right questions.

LUCI SWINDOLL
AUTHOR AND SPEAKER

As society changes the roles we as women play, many of us are left searching for something, something we cannot quite grasp or define. In Designing a Woman's Life *Judy Couchman guides us through looking at our lives and most importantly God's individual direction for us. I especially appreciated her wisdom in the area of discovering and defining our life purpose, which has been a valuable exercise in my own life. For every woman who is searching for her place in today's world,* Designing a Woman's Life *provides a road map.*

MARITA LITTAUER
AUTHOR AND SPEAKER

Designing a Woman's Life *is full of the kind of gutsy honesty that has become Judy Couchman's trademark. But this book also radiates a new poise and maturity. Warm and wise, this book will both encourage and challenge women to find focus and purpose in their busy lives.*

MAXINE HANCOCK, PH.D.
AUTHOR AND SPEAKER

How refreshing to find a book so full of practical, professional, emotional, and biblical insights that help me put in perspective God's unique design for me! I've laughed with it and cried with it. It has challenged me, affirmed me, exhorted me, and admonished me. Judy's poignant personal and biblical illustrations captured the heart of how women struggle with "doing" versus "being." This is a must read for "busy women" who desire to understand their significance and purpose and to embrace their potential for God.

KATHE L. WUNNENBERG
EXECUTIVE DIRECTOR,
CHRISTIAN BUSINESS WOMEN'S ASSOCIATION
PHOENIX, AZ

Designing a
Woman's Life

DESIGNING A WOMAN'S LIFE

Discovering Your Unique
Purpose and Passion

JUDITH COUCHMAN

MULTNOMAH BOOKS
SISTERS, OREGON

DESIGNING A WOMAN'S LIFE

published by Multnomah Books
a part of the Questar publishing family

© 1995 by Judy C. Couchman

International Standard Book Number: 0-88070-837-9

Cover photo by Jim Vecchione
Cover design by David Carlson

Printed in the United States of America
Most Scripture quotations are from:
The Holy Bible, New International Version (NIV)
© 1973, 1984 by International Bible Society,
used by permission of Zondervan Publishing House

Also quoted:
The King James Version (KJV)

The Message, © 1993 by Eugene H. Peterson

The Amplified Bible
© 1987 by The Zondervan Corporation
and The Lockman Foundation

98 99 00 01 02 — 10 9 8 7 6 5

For my nieces:
Catherine, Melissa, Kristine.
May each grow into the woman
she's designed to be.

So nigh is grandeur to our dust,
So near is God to man,
When Duty whispers low, Thou must,
The youth replies, I can.

RALPH WALDO EMERSON

Contents

Acknowledgments

How do I adequately thank the people who granted me the wish of a lifetime? This book represents two decades of listening to thinking women and wrestling with how to infuse biblical principles into their frazzled lives. As a result, I've longed to write a simple treatise that encourages women to ignite with spiritual purpose and passion.

I hope this book is finally it. For its publication I thank Carol Bartley, Rebecca Price, and Dan Rich at Questar for their unwavering belief in my sketchy outline and vague explanations. Carol, my editor, especially exercised faith and ran up telephone bills listening to my ramblings about God, women, and the universe as I thought through this manuscript and rewrote chapters. Carol, you are one of the best.

Thanks also to Janet Guy for her careful research assistance and to Deena Davis, Madalene Harris, and Susan Pannell for reading the raw manuscript and providing feedback.

I am also grateful and indebted to the *Clarity* magazine prayer team, whose members fell so deep into my life they covenanted to pray about Everything Concerning Judith instead of just that publication. Along with my mother, Opal Couchman, her friend Mae Lammers, and my sister Shirley Honeywell, these women prayed for this book: Charette Barta, Win Couchman, Madalene Harris, Karen Hilt, and Nancy Lemons. May you feel their prayers and the Holy Spirit's presence as you read these pages.

Reflection

Designing a Life Worth Living

*I began these pages for myself, in order to think out my own
particular pattern of living, my own individual balance of life,
work and human relationships. And since I think best with
a pencil in my hand, I started naturally to write.*

ANNE MORROW LINDBERGH

IT IS THE NIGHT after my niece's high-school graduation. We sit in
a French restaurant, probably more my taste than hers, to celebrate this
juncture that ushers her deeper into womanhood. I feel proud. She
seems weary from the emotion of saying good-bye to schoolmates and
the tradition of staying up all night after grasping a diploma.

I am unabashedly honored by Melissa's presence tonight, that
despite her fatigue, she spends these hours with me. In the cafe's
shadows her round, chocolate eyes look more alluring, the gentleness
of her personality seems more charming. *No wonder the boys adore*

her, I catch myself thinking and try not to wonder if any young man will prove worthy of this special niece.

As she talks, I search those eyes that despite sleeplessness brim with expectation for the days and years ahead. She anticipates new adventures, full of dreams that without a doubt to her will surely blossom. She, though just across a food-crowded table, sits firmly on the brink of possibilities.

I, on the other side, savoring the salmon, totter toward midlife. Here at last I admit it. Until now I've kept myself busy enough—and perhaps steeped in enough denial—to ignore its swaggering approach. But tonight forces me to admit that the toddler who once clung to my words now creates plans of her own, without my advice. And that eighteen years have passed since I gazed into her newborn crib and cried because I was leaving home to catch dreams.

Along with Melissa I have grown older. As the elder I pressure myself to say wise and memorable words to her, to release her into adulthood with confidence and security, but the syllables catch in my throat. Suddenly uneasy with my senior status I fear sounding bossy or condescending or, God forbid, old-fashioned. So I give up before I begin and am relieved just to talk, to laugh, to applaud her.

After all, we ventured here to celebrate.

Days later, alone in my house miles away, I think again of the con-trasts between my niece and me. As she starts to explore, I welcome the need to focus. As she scoops up activities, I long to lay some down. As she considers umpteen destinations, I steady my slowing self on a narrowing path.

I admit that Melissa's youth tempts me toward nostalgia, but if given the chance, would I return to young adulthood? Probably not. Despite its zest and opportunity, I treasure the self-assurance developed through years of living. But all told, neither youth nor midlife proves more glorious than the other; each life place reveals its foibles and fortitudes; each flows along the natural course of human maturity. Each secretly, if not openly, harbors the desire for purpose and meaning.

So in an almost unnoticed yet poignant way, my niece's path converges with mine. She has joined me on the journey of womanhood, searching for what it means to be female and to become herself. These are ageless tasks. Multitudes of women travel these roads, hoping to unfold a map that spares them the silent terror of barely groping along. We long for more than mere existence. We wonder whether in this lifetime we will discover our unique purpose, our reason for being, and as practicalities and responsibilities increase, whether we will uncover the time—even a few secluded moments—to ponder such other worldly ideas.

This commonality binds women together; this heart cry prompts me to write. After years of searching I believe a woman of faith can know and pursue and relish her unique mission in life. As with most authors, my ideas flow easier on paper. So in this location, in this manner, I write about womanhood: about creating a meaningful life, about unearthing the true person within, about making a difference in this uncertain world. About living with purpose and passion.

First, I write for my lovely niece, with the hope she can avoid discovering herself too late in life. Already in her I sense a yearning for significance that without gentle guidance could be snuffed out as obligations increasingly invade her. Next, I write for myself, to ponder and realign my own pattern of living which, midst the pressure of the daily and mundane, too often falls off track from what I truly think and believe. Then when this manuscript finds a readership, I write for the everywoman who desires clarity of purpose and vision in her day-to-day living.

Yet contrary to books of recent years, these pages won't fill with how-tos and goal-setting lists. (How tired we've grown of always doing, doing, doing.) Rather, the chapters travel a more reflective, fundamental landscape. They explore values, character, and spirituality. They speak of looking within and molding the shape of our souls.

And most important, they focus on being, then doing. For that is how we escape mere existence and design a purposeful life, a life worth living.

Chapter One

Significance

Embracing Our Innate Worth

*To me, one of the proofs that God's hand is behind and
all throughout this marvelous Book we know as the Bible is the
way it continually touches upon this very fear in us—the fear
that we are so insignificant as to be forgotten. That we are nothing.
Unconsciously, His Word meets this fear, and answers it.*

AMY CARMICHAEL

THIS MORNING my house looks like a tornado of two-year-olds hit it.

In the kitchen and dining room, stacks of dirty dishes pile every
which way with no regard for order or cleanliness. The stairway and
living room carpets glisten with multicolored glitter, gold and silver
sequins, and shreds of metallic streamers.

Meandering through the first floor, still wearing a bathrobe and
sipping Viennese coffee, I survey the debris and mentally pronounce my
study as the biggest disaster. Globs of glue stick to a teak worktable

piled high with gift paper, pipe cleaners, squares of felt, bows and ribbons, assorted-sized buttons, valentine stickers, and a variety of cherub-shaped decorations. I count eleven bottles of glue and twelve rolls of Scotch tape. Wads of wrapping tissue nestle between a chair's legs, and hundreds of tiny, shiny lips and hearts smile up at me from the Oriental rug.

Any other self-respecting perfectionist might feel upset, but I just chuckle at the mess as I recall the activity that produced it. Yesterday I hosted a Valentine's Day luncheon for friends—about two dozen women ranging in age from thirtyish to late sixties. These women created the clutter, but they also forged a wonderful memory.

After serving an English tea, I gathered them together and explained the Sunday afternoon project. Calling attention to the decorations stacked in my study, I asked that each woman create a valentine's bag (in lieu of the traditional box) to hold the greeting cards she would receive during this loving holiday. The women displayed no reticence. Singles and marrieds, mothers and grandmothers, homemakers and career women dug through the creative possibilities and like young girls, laughed their way through my Decorating the Bags ritual.

My friends' creativity and originality astonished me as I noticed each woman's personality expressed in her paper bag's design. A die-hard romantic constructed an angel blowing kisses; a pregnant woman poured tissue streamers out of her bag's mouthlike stomach; an analytical artist's creation proclaimed "Love Stinks." Another woman joked that, not unlike her, the cherub on her bag sported a crooked halo. (I thought this was funny until I discovered she'd named the cherub Judy.) Every creation fascinated me, and a judge awarded chocolate prizes for the most clever, most romantic, and most decorated bags.

After dessert and passing out valentine cards, my friends bade good-bye and returned home to their adult responsibilities, but their childlike pleasure lingers. This morning I've received phone calls from several women, describing their joy over yesterday afternoon. What created such feeling? To borrow some of their vernacular, "yammering with girlfriends" and "scarfing up great food" contributed to the satisfaction. But I think the real reason runs deeper. These women tapped into the joy of creating, but even more, they expressed their individuality.

The Need for Expression

After two decades of professionally interacting with and writing for women, I'm convinced the desire for self-expression lies deep within the female soul. At times we may repress it, call it selfishness, or not recognize it poised in our path, but nonetheless the need for expression, both verbal and nonverbal, persists almost in spite of ourselves.

On the surface we express ourselves by what we wear, how we decorate our homes, whom we claim as friends, how we train our children, how we fashion sentences, and other ordinary ways. Unfortunately these means of expression can sometimes remain unacknowledged or unappreciated because they rotate around the familiar and utilitarian. A famished child doesn't care about the creative placement of his food; the exhausted husband may not notice a rearranged living room; a demanding boss can forget to compliment the precise detail; a busy neighbor may not catch our subtle humor. But despite inattention and the occasional frustration it produces in us, we can't help but express ourselves. God modeled humanity after himself, and he perpetually expresses his personality through creation.

Still, these are pragmatic self-proclamations; we accomplish them in the obvious realm of the everyday without much thought or consequence. Below the surface, however, lies an even deeper yearning for expression that springs from our desire for meaning and a "reason for being" in the world. We long to understand and express our unique purpose. In our rare quiet moments we implore, "Does my life have meaning?" and many of us hear emptiness instead of answers.

The silence does not mean the Creator ignores these queries. It's more likely we're too harried to listen to his reply or don't understand how to hear his voice. Or we miss the apparent signs in a search for the mystical and mysterious. Certainly a spiritual quest plays an indisputable role in discovering and expressing our purpose, but so does the commonplace. Yet when pursuing our purpose, neither of these emerge as the starting point. Rather, discovering our purpose begins with embracing our relationship to God as precious, unrepeatable individuals whom he cherishes. Before we "do" our purpose, we need an unshakable belief in his love and our significance to him, for without this stabilizing foundation, we can pursue tasks and priorities that crumble to meaninglessness.

However, with this foundation we can face the pressures of fulfilling our purpose and not waste spiritual energy questioning, "Does what I do matter?" or "Should I be taking this path?" We already know the yes answer.

His Love, Our Significance

Since the beginning of time individuals have wondered aloud about humanity's significance and without figuring God into the equation, have reached disappointing conclusions. After drifting from Jehovah, King Solomon, who possessed riches, power, honor, wisdom, and reputation, told his subjects, "Utterly meaningless! Everything is meaningless."[1]

Nearly three thousand years later historian Carl Becker echoed this sentiment to our generation: "The significance of man is that he is that part of the universe that asks the question, What is the significance of man?... The significance of man is that he is insignificant and is aware of it."[2]

Searchers looked to both of these men for wisdom, but according to their best advice, where do we wind up? Indecipherable specks clinging to a global-warming, war-invoking, ever-whirling universe. If this is Truth, then stop the world, we need to jump off. Who we are and what we do hold no meaning because we are insignificant, and eventually we begin to question our daily routine and very existence. Why pull weeds, change diapers, peck at a computer, cook another meal, or review corporate ledgers for one more day? Why reason with squabbling siblings or paint with watercolors? Without underlying significance we possess no rationale, no modus operandi, for tackling anything, so why try? We might as well grab some junk food and spend our days staring at a larger-than-life television screen. And sadly that's what many women feel like doing.

Fortunately when we hold a biblical worldview, we need not accept this life sentence. It is narrow, stifling, futile. Most of all, it is untrue. It contradicts the sacred Scriptures, which describe God as the loving Shepherd who "gathers the lambs in his arms and carries them close to his heart."[3] David, another biblical king, asked, "When I consider your heavens, the work of your fingers, the moon and the stars, which you have set in place, what is man that you are mindful of him, the son of man that you care for him? You made him a little lower than the heavenly beings and crowned him with glory and honor."[4]

These statements point to humanity's importance to God, but what about our individual and personal significance to him? It's far easier to recognize our worth as collective human beings (maybe the geniuses and famous names and humanitarians will upgrade our own doubtful status) than to stand alone and announce, "By myself I am significant. I am irreplaceable to God."

But remarkably, this is the truth.

The Scriptures call each of us the apple of God's eye[5] and individuals he's hovered over since our days in the womb.[6] So even when we recognize our "smallness" compared to the unending universe, we can still resonate with Mother Teresa of Calcutta who says, "Millions and millions must be in His hand, and yet He can see me—right there in His hand! I must be a very small particle somewhere, but must be there because He says so."[7]

God not only holds us in his hand, but another biblical metaphor depicts him as the loving parent who promises, "Can a mother forget the baby at her breast and have no compassion on the child she has borne? Though she may forget, I will not forget you!"[8] In other words, God the eternal Creator desires to cultivate an intimate, lifelong love relationship with each of us. This is why he sent Jesus to atone for our sins and break the barrier between humanity and the holy, why he saves us from eternal death by his grace and not by our works, why as the Hound of Heaven he doggedly pursues us.[9]

This is unfathomable significance.

A Simple, Loving Reality

My mother still beams when she repeats this story from my oldest sister's childhood. It varies a bit with each telling, but the message remains constant. Whenever Shirley returned home from kindergarten or another outing without Mom, she marched into the house and yelled, "I'm here!" This announcement signaled my mother's part in the routine: she fawned over her daughter's presence.

Mom had no trouble with her role in the performance. This young child issued from her blood; this Shirley Temple look-alike sprang from her loving procreation. How could she not delight in her daughter's existence? Any other response would have been utterly unthinkable. Nearly fifty years later, Mother still feels this joy for her children and grandchildren. Though she encourages and revels in our accomplishments, more than anything Mom loves us just because we belong to her.

This, too, is the way of God the Father. He declares to his children, "I have loved you with an everlasting love."[10] He draws us to himself for the sheer pleasure of it. He loves us not for who we are, or what we do, or who we can or will be. He loves us because he created us, because we belong to him.

It is a profoundly simple reality.

It is especially difficult for women to own this reality for ourselves, even if we are mothers, or adult children blessed with parents exceedingly talented at loving. We base our significance on doing and hope the activity will verify our value and lovability. We do not easily understand that just being a person created by God makes us deeply significant.

However, when we're willing to wrestle with our disbelief and eventually embrace this significance, when we push beyond an intellectual understanding into the knowledge of the heart, it poignantly influences how we view ourselves and manage our lives. Instead of questioning our worth and berating our imperfections, we can consider ourselves magnificent works of art in progress, filled with meaning and the freedom to be whom God created us to be.

We can be like the beautiful work of art that sits in my upstairs bedroom, the kind that beckons attention, evokes emotion, and lingers in the mind. It is an exquisite piece of pottery that woos and teases passersby. Half vase because of its small pedestal bottom and half pot due to its wide girth and mouth, this creation embodies the word *unique*. On one side the wavy edged mouth dips into a slit, creating a feminine, slightly sexy effect enhanced by the pot's muted peach, tan, and white colors.

I would admire this intriguing artwork no matter what, but it's especially meaningful because my friend Pat thoughtfully shaped the piece and presented it to me as a birthday gift. It serves as a monument to our friendship.

A narrow-eyed pragmatist might examine this creation and question, "What good is it? It doesn't do anything." And yes, I could fill the pot with pine cones or tennis balls or jewelry or whatever—just to assign it something to do—but that would detract from its intrinsic beauty. All things considered, I value the pottery's form more than its function.

This is how God feels about us. We are his beautiful and thoughtful creation. Like one-of-a-kind pottery, above all else he treasures our innate worth. We are immensely significant, and our value does not depend on anything we do, think, say, feel, earn, inherit, or look like. It is because we exist as God's creation. Finis. Nothing more.

When we internalize this principle, we can accomplish nothing or everything admired by the human race (within biblical parameters) and keep peace within our souls. We hear the Creator's affirming whispers and know that our significance does not fluctuate with the circum-stances. We stay God-centered and internally free. We find ourselves rooted in love and confidence instead of tossed by the wavering winds of accomplishment.

The Trappist monk Thomas Merton wrote of this rootedness in his book *The New Man*. He explained: "Man 'finds himself' and is happy, when he is able to be aware that his freedom is spontaneously and vigorously functioning to orientate his whole being toward the purpose which it craves, in its deepest spiritual center, to achieve. This purpose is *life* in the fullest sense of the word—not mere indi-vidual, self-centered, egotistical life which is doomed to end in death, but a life that transcends individual limitations and needs, and subsists outside the individual self in the Absolute—in Christ, in God."[11]

"Subsisting in God" does not demand that we stop our lives, give up thinking, and flee to the desert for a lifetime of solitude, though at times this sounds appealing. Unlike my bedroom pottery which sits endlessly, God gives his children tasks to complete. Even in Eden he assigned the first man and woman the job of tending a garden. But understanding our significance before we attempt accomplishment anchors the soul in an order uncommon to this world. First, we embrace our innate worth, then we pursue our unique purpose. After this, we tackle our work.

Because we live in imperfect bodies in a broken world, our work, whether domestic or in the marketplace, will meet with opposition and disappointment, so embracing our significance protects us from shattering when our occupation changes or dissipates. That is, when God allows circumstances to point our life journey in a direction that we do not want, plan, or expect, our inner security doesn't crumble. We focus on him first, then everything else falls into perspective. This means that whatever life serves us—times of productivity or seasons of fallowness, Olympian flexibility or confinement to a wheelchair, personal and professional highs or lows—we define ourselves by our significance to God rather than by what we do.

The Glorious Irony

Probably the most searing examples of individuals who understood their innate significance are the Christian martyrs. In the book *By Their Blood* for nearly six hundred pages James and Marti Hefley recount the stories of twentieth-century believers who, though persecuted, murdered, or debilitated by disease, considered it an honor to suffer for God even when their work yielded no visible success.

After the Boxer rebellion in China and the slaughter of countless Christians, missionary Mrs. A. B. Magnuson wrote in a letter: "Looking back on our work in Mongolia it seems dark, having borne little

fruit, but I lift my eyes upward to Him who can look deeper and far-
ther than we can look and does not judge simply by the outward
appearance as we do. He can change and transform all things and no
work for Him is in vain."[12]

Apparently Mrs. Magnuson sought and followed her purpose in
life—she worked at doing what God designed for her—but she stayed
grounded in her significance to him. She kept spiritually centered
despite murderous circumstances and what looked like failure.

In contrast, most of us won't live out our faith in a foreign country, in front of a literal firing squad. We wrestle with our significance
over loads of laundry, with controlling bosses, in sputtering marriages,
during threatening illnesses, in the midst of tough college courses and
other day-in and day-out scenarios. Our search for significance back-
drops against a culture that expects activity and perfection, yet delivers
addiction and disappointment.

As unbelievable as it seems, our plight is no less important to
God than Mrs. Magnuson's and the martyrs'. God desires for all of his
children to own their significance to him, to learn that before their
Creator they matter. When we truly understand this concept, everyone
else's opinion of us and our work pales in comparison.

Once we grasp this principle, a glorious irony emerges. When we
rest in God's love and our significance to him, we naturally desire to
please the one who so unconditionally accepts us; we long to discover
and complete his life task for us. We can pursue this task, this purpose,

with a fresh abandonment that concerns itself with following the Creator instead of being a "success" or "failure" in the world's judgmental eyes or according to the voice of our internal critic. When we feel accepted for being who we are, we are unafraid to do what we're created to do. We become like children at play, risking everything and imagining anything because a loving parent protectively watches us from nearby.

I've observed this childlike approach to risk in my friend Susan. In the midst of a frustrating job situation, she plunged into understanding her significance to God. At the time I was so wrapped up in my work that the concept didn't interest me, so her decisions looked alarming. Susan quit her corporate job and launched a business, but more than that she deliberately focused on God's acceptance of her. As a result she burst with creativity and a risk taking in relationships that has deeply touched her friends. Susan modeled to me how embracing our innate worth enhances what we do.

Taking the Big Leap

If we at least faintly desire to embrace our innate worth, how do we start? It seems a long jump over the chasm between our gnawing uncertainties and such lavish self-esteem.

Although we'd prefer receiving step-by-step instructions from someone who already has mastered this principle, the learning process doesn't operate that way. It unfolds itself differently for each individual, and another simple reality confronts us at this point. As with everything else in life, we are not the ultimate controllers of this learning process. God is. We can pray, meditate on Scripture, and listen to other people's stories, or attend seminars and Bible studies. But the most important action is *simply to ask God to reveal the truth to us in the manner he chooses.*

When we express a willingness to learn, God allows individual circumstances to teach us about our true worth, and when we release ourselves to his wisdom and trustworthiness, recognizing and cooperating with the process, the leap to significance grows less frightening. He often uses unexpected and unwanted changes in circumstances to expose our misplaced beliefs and priorities.

This last statement reminds me of Gwen. Instead of attending our Thanksgiving feast last year, she lay in the hospital recovering from a hysterectomy and a sobering diagnosis: ovarian cancer and possibly a shortened life. This, after leaving a painful job, surviving a divorce, moving to another state, gaining new employment, and building a house. "Why is this happening?" we asked one another while missing her presence at the dinner table. "Why, when her life is just getting put back together?"

Two months later we recreated the Thanksgiving meal at Gwen's house (one should never miss a celebration), and she astonished us all. Poised and beautiful, Gwen's serenity put our petty problems in their place. She exemplified grace under pressure.

Gwen admits she hasn't always handled life this well. A recovering workaholic, she once built her significance on her job, her husband and children, her creative home, even her health. But when one by one these fell away, circumstances led Gwen to move her God-based significance from an intellectual to an experiential knowledge. Recently she told me, "You know, I think I'm finally learning it. Life isn't about what we do; it's about who we are." I'm not suggesting that God caused Gwen's upheavals, but I do offer this: for reasons often beyond our comprehension, he uses life's problems to teach us about our true value.

This also happened to me. For about a decade I cradled a dream to launch a magazine for contemporary Christian and spiritually seeking women, a magazine that would sidestep pat answers and stereotypes to stimulate their thinking about God. As I traveled the country and talked to women, they expressed their hunger for such a publication, but more important, the Spirit of God wooed me with this destiny.

A good start, but from there I tried wresting the dream from God's hands (which I discovered is impossible), functioned as though everything depended solely upon me, and agonized about the implausibility of it all. I had no money or other means to start the periodical's development, not even a job that would foster it. I later learned that money and positioning proved a cinch compared to the overhaul and preparation of my heart. Throughout my soul I'd threaded the belief that my significance depended upon accomplishment and exterior possessions. The translation: if the magazine launched, this would prove me a woman of significance. If it never launched or failed after its introduction, I would be worth little or nothing.

When through a series of miracles the magazine project finally entered the research and development phase, I worked maniacally and reached a state of exhaustion and depression. Then, and only then, I released the project to God's care and focused on healing myself. I remember the pivotal day when I declared this manifesto: "I am not *Clarity* magazine. Whether it lives or dies, as an individual I am deeply valuable to God. My work is not my identity."

All of this learning occurred in the fire-filled belly of everyday life. I believe God teaches us our most profound lessons there, for it is in everyday situations and relationships that we must apply them. Stripped down and feeling the heat, we evaluate the true meaning of significance.

Learning Sooner Than Later

I don't expect every woman's experience to mimic mine or Susan's or Gwen's. In fact, I would prefer that we didn't need to feel pain before accepting God's truth about ourselves, that without difficulty most of us could perceive and believe in our real significance apart from friends, health, family, beauty, status, and accomplishment. But the human will is wily, and I suspect each person faces at least one individually shaped crisis before learning the truth. It seems the most reliable way to move this concept from head to heart knowledge.

My prayer is that women will learn this sooner than later, for living and working without spiritually based significance shrinks the soul. Jesus asked, "What good will it be for a man if he gains the whole world, yet forfeits his soul?"[13] He (or she) finds no meaning in life.

Months ago I briefly explained the core of this chapter to a thoughtful friend. "Sounds interesting, but I have a question," she replied. "Judy, can a woman in her twenties internalize this concept, without having lived as long or accomplished as much as a woman in her forties or fifties?"

It's possible but, given our culture and nature, it could be less probable. We pressure young women to produce—attend college, choose a career, get married, give life to babies—and the idea of innate worth doesn't occur to them much; they are busy with the heady newness of *doing*. But after life tosses us around for a while, we wonder about significance and search for ways to redefine ourselves.

However, with God's supernatural touch, I believe young women can embrace this concept. I long for women of all ages—twenty-five or forty-two or seventy-six—to internalize their innate worth and then ascend to their unique purpose. I know women who've embraced this significance in their twenties. I know women in their seventies who've never tried. With God, it is never too early and never too late, not only to understand our significance but to discover our purpose.

Today is the day to begin.

Chapter Two

Purpose

Finding Our God-Intended Destiny

[God] has given each of us the gift of life with a specific purpose in view.
To Him work is a sacrament, even what we consider
unimportant, mundane work....
For each of us, He does have a plan.
What joy to find it and even out of our helplessness,
let Him guide us in its fulfillment.

CATHERINE MARSHALL

IF A CHURCH BUILDING is our definition of God's house, then we'll probably reconsider and grant him more living space after meeting Gena.

Nearly sixty years old and formidable in both presence and purpose, Gena insists that she manages God's house, which in this case is a dark, brick building on Mount Eden Parkway in the Bronx, New York. She fills up the house with homeless people, feeding them, doling out beds, and above all, ensuring that her come-and-go boarders show respect for the unseen but never forgotten heavenly host.

"They cain't practice religion in my house," announces Gena and then elaborates on her no-nonsense hospitality. "If they a Muslim, I say what happened to Allah when you needed a bed? Is he on vacation? Is he asleep? When you in my God's house, eating my God's food, you show Him respect."

Gena also commands respect, but not just from the streetwise men and women who temporarily inhabit her labyrinth of floors and rooms. The neighbors, the police, the churches, the prisons, the hospitals— they all know that the Mount Eden Rescue Mission and its proprietor help people straighten up their lives. A sign above the door declares, "This is a drug-free building. Violators will forfeit their freedom," and Gena means it. She prohibits sexual activity between guests and turns out visitors with weapons, saying, "I ain't never put nobody out. You put yourselves out." And for every rule breaker who exits, another misplaced person enters and promises to play it straight.

For Gena, playing it straight etches the fragile line between life and death. This is a dangerous, unpredictable neighborhood that doesn't necessarily return a well-intentioned woman's hospitality. "God better call you to this, I tell you one thing, or the devil will kill you in a minute," she says. "Some woman started up a place down the street, and didn't she get murdered? You can't be wanting anything or depending on anything but the name of Jesus in this business, no sir. We on the straight and narrow, honey. When you on this road, you gotta grease down."

The talk may sound tough, but Gena's heart stays soft. Family members say she's always taken people into her home. Even as a young mother with four children, she usually had somebody extra sleeping on the floor. "Couldn't we have one Thanksgiving with just our family?" complained the kids, but their mama provided for the homeless even before turning to Christ at a tent meeting over twenty years ago.

For a time after her conversion Gena asked God to give her a ministry, while she kept opening her home to an assortment of needy people. Then she realized he had already ingrained an outreach in her bones, and with this conviction Gena's Thanksgiving swelled to sixty or seventy people rather than six or seven. Some might say at this point a ministry ignited, but actually Gena just stoked up a low-burning flame and fanned it toward society's unwanted: crack addicts, con artists, alcoholics, unwed mothers, the helpless and hopeless.

It's not easy. But for Gena, it's right.

"People getting sick of the homeless," she says. "When I first opened this place, they was rich folks, white folks, asking what can we do? Now they sick of it. I'll tell you, these demons come here with an attitude. They say, 'Give me breakfast, and hurry up!' I don't feel sorry for them—they's wicked—on drugs and alcohol mostly. I am motivated by Jesus Christ. If I wasn't, I'd throw water in their faces."

Even then, I imagine she'd be splashing around holy water, for Gena offers her work, her life, as a sacrament.[1]

Desperately Seeking Purpose

With her brusque style Gena hardly fits some people's stereotype of a Christian woman, yet it's her unapologetic individuality that captures the heart. The women I know who've encountered Gena in person or in print confess to feeling profoundly affected by her determined, even forceful, sense of mission and almost in the same breath mutter something about wishing they possessed a certainty about their own purpose.

These comments have led me to ask, *Why are there so few women like Gena who, no matter how menial or frustrating or monumental the task, consider their lives and work a sacred trust from God?* The irony struck me recently while perusing bookstores for quotes and stories about females who from an internal sense of God-intended direction knew they made a difference in the world. I could barely find a handful. My own library brims with hardbacks about women who created personal and professional legacies—actors, authors, aviators, comics, dancers, homekeepers, mothers, musicians, philosophers, politicians, psychologists, rulers, social activists—but unfortunately these women, though successful from a secular viewpoint, pursued purposes apart from the Creator's guidance and sold their souls for it.

So why didn't women who claim a personal relationship with God show up on the shelves? If they embrace their significance to God, shouldn't believers be the most purposeful, fulfilled, and influential women in the world? I admit that a biography is no indicator of a person's true success, but still, where were the spiritually attuned achievers? I hoped the lack represented the publishing world's mind-set rather than a symptom of female purposelessness.

Then I thought about how the Scriptures speak of Christians living "peaceful and quiet lives in all godliness and holiness."[2] Perhaps this indicated where to find the purpose-filled, spiritually alive women: in their homes, at their jobs, around the community. Not calling attention to themselves, dodging the desire for fame, but nonetheless pursuing their unique destinies in quiet and meaningful ways. So I sorted through the many women I've known—past and present—through friendship, social interaction, work associations, even conferences. Yes, they kept busy. Yes, they'd accomplished. But if the conversation rolled around to it, many privately admitted a gnawing need for something more. They wanted to know *exactly why* God placed them on the earth and *specifically what* they were to be doing. They were still searching for purpose.

It has been a sobering realization, this pent-up meaninglessness, this lack of understood destiny that characterizes so many women's lives, but it does not leave me hopeless. With God all things are possible,[3] and that includes each of us assuredly pursuing our purpose and passion in life.

The Meaning of Purpose

We can't find something if we don't know what we're looking for, so it's essential to define purpose before launching out after it. An obvious fact, but one that often gets overlooked in a flurry of enthusiasm that plunges first and thinks later, after hitting a few walls. And what could prompt more excitement than the possibility of uncovering our unique purpose? What could be more inviting, more joyous, than growing into everything we're created to be, fulfilling the life we're meant to live?

Simply defined, purpose is "the object for which something exists or is done; [the] end in view," and to do something "on purpose" is to tackle it "by design" or intentionally.4 So from a spiritual standpoint, pursuing our purpose means *to discover our God-intended reason for being and to design our lives accordingly.* This uncomplicated definition requires the length and breadth of a lifetime to thoroughly understand it, but it begins clearly enough: to discover our reason for being.

With his booklet *How to Find Your Mission in Life,* Richard Bolles suggests we have not just one, but three purposes or reasons for being in life and each one requires mastery before approaching the next. Briefly these purposes are to live in the presence of God, to make this world a better place, and to exercise our greatest talent for God's work in the world.5 Although this book focuses on the third purpose, the first two purposes merit a short exploration because they build a foundation for the outflow of our giftedness.

Living in God's Presence

The Westminster catechism asks the question, "What is the chief and highest end of man?" and provides the still relevant answer: "Man's chief and highest end is to glorify God, and fully to enjoy Him for-ever."[6] In basic terms this is what it means to fulfill the first purpose, to live in the presence of God. Our first priority revolves around knowing God; we spend time relating to him before we begin doing for him. Intimacy before action.

For women like me who've based their significance on what they've accomplished, this purpose statement sends something akin to shock through us. It sounds so passive, so devoid of the thrill of the hunt. But the Bible repeatedly advises us to love God with all our heart, soul, and strength and to seek his kingdom first so "all these things will be given to [us] as well."[7] In other words, we must intimately know the Purpose-Giver so we can express his purpose through us, so his pur-pose becomes our own.

A gifted actor or dancer practices this principle. She spends many hours researching and rehearsing and soaking in her subject so in a per-formance the audience no longer sees the performer but rather the person or thing she represents. In her first autobiography the celebrated ballerina Gelsey Kirkland tells of dancing the part of a female insect in the ballet *The Cage*. During one practice session Gelsey and her coach dropped to the studio floor and hunted for cockroaches to assist them in understanding the movement of her character. Later Gelsey advanced to observing the praying mantis, and only after days of studying and practicing could she execute authentic movements that made "dance sense."[8] And all so she could represent a bug.

In regard to our creative representation of God to the world, where does the ballerina's example leave us? How well do we study the Creator so when we play out our first purpose before the world people see him instead of us? As for me, I have miles to travel before people see Jesus rather than me in my life and work.

Making a Better World

While the first purpose centers on our relationship with God, the second purpose—to make the world a better place—addresses our interaction with his creation and particularly humans, both the spiritually believing and unbelieving. Yet even cola commercials sing of making the world a better place, so how do we make a God-inspired difference on humanity?

When referring to his people, the Lord rhetorically asked Moses, "What does the LORD your God ask of you?" Then he continued: "to fear [respect or reverence] the LORD your God, to walk in [obey] all his ways, to love him, to serve the LORD your God with all your heart and with all your soul, and to observe the LORD's commands."9

To respect, to obey, to love, to serve—these actions when practiced with a heart bowed to the Spirit's guidance develop holy character within us and draw people to new life in God. But again, these actions flow toward God first, then move out to others.

After surviving the horrors of Ravensbrück, a German concentration camp, and losing her father and sister to Hitler's atrocities, Corrie ten Boom embarked on a speaking ministry that took her around the world. Over and over, Corrie spoke of God's faithfulness during her imprisonment. As a motivating slogan for the arduous days of travel and ministry, she chose the phrase "Not good if detached," patterned after an instruction printed on a train ticket. She explained, "Connected with Jesus, His victory is my victory. Not good if detached from Him." [10]

Eventually Corrie returned to Germany—a difficult step for apparent reasons. At a meeting in a friend's house, she noticed a woman who would not look her in the eye. Corrie asked her hostess about the woman and discovered she had worked as a nurse at Ravensbrück. Suddenly Corrie recognized the woman and filled with hate. Ten years before, Corrie had escorted her sister Betsie to the camp's hospital barracks. Betsie's feet were paralyzed, and Corrie knew her sister was dying. But instead of expressing sympathy the nurse scolded Betsie.

During the meeting Corrie wrestled with her decade-old bitterness and finally asked God for forgiveness. She wanted to stay attached to his purposes. The next day, with a supernatural love welling within, Corrie telephoned the woman and invited her to another session that night.

"What? Do *you* want *me* to come?" gasped the nurse.

"Yes," replied Corrie. "That is why I called you."

"Then I'll come."

That night during the meeting, the nurse looked Corrie directly in the eye and afterwards committed her life to Christ.

Corrie faced similar experiences on several occasions and explained the phenomena this way: "I, who have kept in my subconsciousness feelings of hatred, the Lord now uses as a window through which His light can shine into [a] dark heart: His channel for streams of living water." [11]

Corrie respected, obeyed, loved, and served—and God fulfilled his redemptive purpose through her. We share this purpose, this serving as God's conduit, with Corrie. In fact the first two purposes, which reduce to knowing God and making him known to others, belong to all of humanity. These purposes prompt us to live according to the Scriptures and develop our character, spirituality, and loving responses in relationships. It is the third purpose—exercising our gifts for God's work in the world—that accentuates a unique and individual contribution to life.

Naming Our Uniqueness

When I consider this third purpose, this desire for uniqueness, I remember the conflicting emotions I felt while attending family reunions as a young girl. On the one hand, I looked forward to visiting the relatives, and now as an adult I can identify the need these gatherings met for me. Aside from filling up on the Midwest's finest fried chicken and fresh-baked pies, the annual pilgrimage to an aunt's house or an uncle's farm instilled within me a sense of belonging and rootedness. For a few days I participated in something bigger than myself, living among people who shared my family history and bore a faint resemblance to me.

On the other hand, too much resemblance made me uncomfortable. My father's siblings would say, "Oh, you look just like a Couchman" and then name the relative, sometimes deceased or unknown to me, whom I favored. Or they pinpointed someone whose talents I'd inherited or attitudes I unwittingly mimicked. After a few of these encounters, I felt myself melting into a pot of family ingredients over which I held no control. While I loved belonging, I disliked being "just like" everyone else. I wanted to be unique, too.

This tension stirs within us over a lifetime. We want to identify with others; we long for personal distinctiveness. We are like other wives, clerks, athletes, mothers, artists, teachers, and executives, but how do we as individuals fill a role and express our giftedness in a way that nobody else does? What would the world miss if we didn't exist? And is it really possible to be one of a kind? These often silent questions expose a universal craving to name our uniqueness. And God, who calls us by name and numbers the hairs on each head,[12] answers our questions with enduring love and patience.

For our need to belong, he reminds us we are his children, bought with a blood-spilled price, members of his family, and heirs to the heavenly kingdom.[13] For our longing to be unique, the psalmist explains God's careful creation of us: "Oh, yes, you shaped me first inside, then out; you formed me in my mother's womb.... You know me inside and out, you know every bone in my body; You know exactly how I was made, bit by bit, how I was sculpted from nothing into something."[14]

If we argue that God sculpted us from a predictable, prefabricated mold, just a look around makes that idea laughable. Though we share similar features such as a head, heart, brain, and limbs, we each possess characteristics that make us unlike any other. Individuals do not think, move, laugh, and approach the myriads of activities called "living" in exactly the same way. Even mothers of identical twins can list the differences between their born-together children.

Look around again, and we discover that throughout creation God juxtaposes not just physical but also spiritual opposites before us. We participate in humanity's sinful nature; we stand individually responsible for accepting redemption. We all belong collectively to God; we each can enjoy a one-to-one relationship with him.[15] We pursue the shared mission of knowing God and making him known; we pursue a purpose that is uniquely our own. The apostle Paul told the Corinthians, "There are different kinds of gifts, but the same Spirit. There are different kinds of service, but the same Lord. There are different kinds of working, but the same God works all of them in all men."[16] God is the unifying force.

I can't think of any combination that secures my heart more than this: as Christians we are bound eternally to God, the parent who loves us unconditionally, and to spiritual brothers and sisters. At the same time we are free—even expected—to exercise our individuality and giftedness in ways that belong only to us. Conformity and creativity.

Belongingness and freedom. Only a mind as masterful as God's could mix these opposites into a harmonious and fulfilling life journey. And it is God whom we can seek when considering which direction to go.

Finding an Overall Direction

I once spoke to a group of California women who meet monthly at seven in the morning to discuss integrating their faith and work. After reeling through a half-hour talk about "Letting God Direct Your Career," I wasn't sure if I'd made sense. (At seven o'clock I am fortunate to stand upright, let alone sound comprehensible.) While packing up my notes and handouts, though, a woman slid alongside me and said, "Thanks for the talk. I now realize what I've been doing wrong. I've been looking for a job instead of seeking a direction."

It intrigued me that the woman gleaned this idea from my speech because finding a life direction and purpose wasn't even the topic. God's Spirit, ever surprising in his approach, must have whispered the truth to her, and I've no doubt that woman will discover her life's purpose. She already understands that when searching for purpose, it's essential to determine a general direction before exploring an exact role or location. But we usually don't approach our lives that way. We ask God, "What job should I take?" or "Which city should I live in?" instead of beginning with the fundamental question, "What overall purpose do you have for my life?" Eager to get on with the program, we try wangling details before contemplating the big picture.

A business consultant will explain that before setting specific goals for a company, the owner or leader and employees need to understand the organization's mission. It is the mission statement—the statement of purpose—that points the people and projects in a harmonious direction; it minimizes confusion, misguided projects, and faulty decisions. It also channels passion and motivation.

A few years ago I listened as friends described their involvement in a new venture within their large company. Whenever they attended a meeting for this project, they left angry and confused—and it took several days for them to recover emotionally from what could have been momentum-building times.

Eventually I asked, "What's making you so upset?"

Both employees replied, "We don't know exactly what the project's purpose is." This lack of mission confused the meetings and frustrated attempts to create new products. Team members disagreed about product development because they had different ideas about direction, so the group fractured and progress stopped. Eventually the group remedied this core problem, but not before losing time, energy, and potential sales.

We may balk at patterning ourselves after corporate structures, but for all their faults successful businesses understand this: projects or people flounder without a specified and articulated purpose. A friend of mine is awakening to this reality. Last week we treated ourselves to a comfort-food lunch because an organization offered another candidate the job she wanted. It stunned us both because Diana is well-qualified, and interviewers had implied she was a sure shot.

After some commiserating about job searches and rejection, I risked applying this book's premise to the situation. (It's hazardous being an author's friend. You can wind up a literary guinea pig or, even worse, an anecdote in a book.)

"Diana, it seems to me that before finding a job, we need to know our purpose," I said. "Do you know your life purpose?"

"No," she replied, looking sad. "Do you know yours?"

Despite several years of friendship it hadn't occurred to me to tell her. Sheepish, I forged ahead. "Yes. It's to publish the glad tidings." Then I explained that a life purpose is a statement of general direction, not an exact job or location. While it provides parameters, it doesn't strap us in tightly and stifle us. In fact, a purpose unleashes creative possibilities.

"There are many ways I can publish the glad tidings," I continued. "As a magazine editor, a book author, even a speaker (the broadest definition of "publish" being "to proclaim or make known"). But this purpose does require that I use my communication skills to encourage people with God's good news. Out of that purpose flow specific jobs, projects, audiences, or locations. So while my purpose remains constant, these other factors give it my unique spin and can change under God's guidance."

We then talked about what makes Diana unique, what delights her, and how these could hint at her life's purpose. Diana's eyes lit up.

Just the thought of pursuing something she intrinsically loved pumped hope into her.

A few days earlier I had a similar conversation with my perennially creative friend Chloe.

"I don't have a lifelong passion like you do," she said.

I couldn't believe it. "But I think you do," I shot back. "Maybe you're thinking too narrowly about defining your purpose. Personally I think your purpose is to create beauty," I said, referring to her interior design business. Chloe reflects God's creative nature by designing beautiful surroundings.

She sat up taller and said, "You might be right!" And I could almost hear her thinking, *Is it okay for a purpose to be something I love?*

Yes. In fact, that is God's intent. He places talents and interests and spiritual gifts within us, then wraps up our purpose in them. It is Satan who tempts us to believe otherwise. He does not appreciate that the Creator is good, and he hates Christians following their spiritual calling and making a profound difference for God in the world. But as the behaviorists say, it will just have to be his problem, not ours. For once we catch a glimpse of ourselves living fully and purposefully, there is no going back. Love and passion propel us forward.

So if we've glimpsed this God-intended destiny, how do we uncover and state our unique and specific purpose?

By digging deeper and staying true to the woman within.

By becoming authentic.

Chapter Three

Authenticity

Staying True to the Woman Within

We can be confident in our uniqueness....
To become the one I am created to be,
isn't that my great work in life?

INGRID TROBISCH

I'LL NEVER FORGET the first time I saw Jan. Lithe and tan and exhilarated from a physical workout, she flashed a smile while hopping off her bike and steering it around me, toward our college dormitory's front door. I don't recall if she said hello, nor can I conjure up our first meaningful conversation, but I do remember feeling refreshed by her unusual beauty and winsome spirit. Her fleeting presence was warm, inviting, almost magical, and immediately I wanted to know her.

Fat chance of that, I thought after she passed by. Based on her demeanor, I surmised she was an upperclassman who'd formerly lived

an intensely popular cheerleader's life somewhere in California. I'd
grown up an introverted Heartland girl who didn't get accepted into
the halls of higher learning for either her good looks or magnetic personality. So it probably bemused our classmates when Jan, who
actually hailed from Michigan and coincidentally bunked in the room
next to mine, turned into one of my college confidantes. At the least,
it surprised me.

I felt even more dumbfounded when one day—each of us
lounging on a rumpled bed—Jan voiced her postgraduate goal to
become a wife and mother. I don't think I told her, but at the time it
seemed such an unremarkable objective for my bright and gifted
friend. After all, we approached adulthood in the early 1970s when
our culture awakened to diversified career choices for women. Even I,
the unnotable student often retiring to the shadows, plotted a future
in journalism, so couldn't Jan become a businesswoman, an environ-
mentalist, or at least fulfill the more traditional role of a teacher?

Absolutely not. Jan followed her heart and after graduation married a man intent on youth ministry, who adored her as much as she
did him, and settled into a modest, domestic lifestyle. I visited her in
their first home, met their toddling daughter, and decades later can still
feel the comforting essence of that Jan-inspired nest.

For several years we corresponded intermittently, but as with most
college friends, the relationship fell prey to annual, one-size-fits-all
Christmas communication. Yet even in those generic letters and photo-
graphs, I read between the lines and sensed the ongoing "rightness" of

Jan's choice. Her inner certainty—despite motherhood's everyday frustrations and the devastating loss of a newborn son—appeared to deepen in proportion to her growing family. And I realized I'd been misguided to think that homemaking was less a career or calling than any other profession.

Last year with Jan's form letter and charming family photo, she jotted a note to congratulate me on the launch of the magazine. Then as an afterthought she added, "Guess I've always been cut out to be a wife and mother." But it was not a statement of self-pity or resignation from a disgruntled woman; it was a declaration of satisfaction over a carefully followed destiny. And even though I'm equally certain and pleased about my purpose, Jan's contentedness rang so true that I momentarily wanted her life.

When it's published, I'll send a copy of this book to Jan, and she'll probably laugh and protest that I've romanticized her, but I also believe she'll agree about the unmistakable presence of quality in her life, a quality based on purposefulness rather than possessions or accomplishments. With the Holy Spirit's guidance, Jan has stayed true to the woman within. She has listened to her soul.

Trusting the Woman Within

When we set out to discover a life purpose, we embark on a journey within, for to understand our reason for being is to recognize the shape of our souls. For Christians, the soul takes shape in God's hand, who indwells the spiritually surrendered believer with his Spirit. When we stay in tune with this Spirit, listening to the woman within can synchronize with hearing from the Creator. But for the Holy Spirit to reveal God's truth in concert with the human soul, we must spiritually plumb our inner person and be convinced that God can and does speak to hearts.

In recent years we've heard much ado about developing the soul and listening to the inner self. But I'm concerned that instead of inspiring biblical believers toward greater internal development, this spiritual talk frightens us. Because much of the rhetoric originates from a hazy spirituality rather than clear-cut Christianity, we bypass even the soulish issues that are scriptural for fear of slipping into the wrong camp and becoming antibiblical. Or at least being accused of scriptural defection.

It's crucial to keep our spirituality centered on a biblical course, but throwing out the proverbial baby with the bathwater can be as damaging as defection. Inattention to the soul drains us of spiritual enlightenment and effectiveness. With internal neglect we grow deaf to God's still, small voice,[1] and we need his whispers to discern our purpose and his guidance.

However, when tending to the soul, defection may not be our deepest fear. We can also avoid looking and listening within because of the sin and unpleasantness we might uncover. Who wants to look within when we could find disobedience, woundedness, indifference, or feelings of inadequacy? Who wants to muster the courage and energy to confront these attitudinal and emotional blockades to our communion with the Holy Spirit? Not many. It's easier to keep the status quo, wrapped in apprehension and bemoaning that we don't know what to do with our lives. Easier, but also unfulfilling and purposeless.

Interesting, isn't it? Children of the compassionate God, the very Creator of our souls, fear looking within ourselves? The operative word here is *fear*. When it emerges, the devil lurks nearby. Fear is his emotional smoke screen, his way of blinding us to God's good will toward us. But God has not given us a spirit of fear, says the Bible. Rather, he imbues us with a spirit of power, love, and self-discipline.[2] When we resist the devil in Christ's name, this power and love banish our blockades and open our souls to the holy mind-set.[3]

"Because the Holy Spirit is today present in His office on earth, all spiritual presence and divine communication of the Trinity with men are via the Spirit," wrote the beloved author Catherine Marshall. "Once the truth of this amazing comradeship gets firmly imbedded in our mind and heart, we need never be afraid again, or lonely, or hopeless, or sorrowful, or helplessly inadequate. For the Helper is always with us, and altogether adequate."[4] Altogether adequate for daily living; fully able to speak to a soul.

When Mary Jane turned to Christ, she quickly devoured the Scriptures and delved deeply into the soul life. More than anyone I've known, she hungered for the Holy Spirit's work within her. One thing concerned me though. Before accepting God's forgiveness, Mary Jane carried on an affair with a married man. Despite her newfound faith, the lover still lingered nearby. I struggled with how to tell Mary Jane that spiritual growth and adultery don't mix, and while I vacillated, the Holy Spirit moved ahead without me.

Actually the Spirit didn't need me at all. As Mary Jane prayed, read the Scriptures, and learned to listen within, she realized the affair was sinful—a barrier to God and his direction for her. She soon ended the relationship, and the last I knew of her she'd grown into a power-ful spiritual intercessor. As an observer of Mary Jane's early spiritual journey, I believe her willingness to listen and obey opened the door to God's purpose for her.

God's word to Mary Jane may be apparent to us, but in more ambiguous situations how do we know we're hearing God's voice and not just our own imagination or temptation from evil forces? The nineteenth century Quaker teacher Hannah Whitall Smith described four timeless ways to discern God's voice. In *The Christian's Secret to a Happy Life,* she explained that God speaks through the Scriptures, providential circumstances, the convictions of our higher judgment, and the inward impressions of the Holy Spirit on our minds. Hannah taught Christians to distinguish God's voice by testing these four influences for harmony.

"His voice will always be in harmony with itself, no matter in how many different ways He may speak." She continued, "The voices may be many, the message can be but one. If God tells me in one voice to do or to leave undone anything, He cannot possibly tell me the opposite in another voice. If there is a contradiction in the voices, the speakers cannot be the same. Therefore my rule for distinguishing the voice of God would be to bring it to the test of this harmony."[5]

These tests can help us learn to trust the woman within.

Cultivating a Relationship

I'm stating the obvious, but it's difficult to recognize someone's voice if we don't cultivate a relationship with that person. When a stranger contacts me by telephone, he'll often call me "Judith" and then state his full name and business or personal association. On the other end of the spectrum, a long-term friend will call me "Judy" (and would laugh at a request to call me "Judith") and can just say "Hi," and I'll know who it is. Years of relationship have attuned me to the nuances of that person's voice and expression.

It is no different with God. The more time we spend with him, the more we sharpen our internal hearing to recognize his voice. We spend this time by reading and obeying Scripture, meditating on the biblically spiritual, communing through asking and listening prayer, journaling our thoughts to and about God, calling upon the Holy Spirit for daily help and wisdom, observing and participating in his work in the world, listening to the holiness in others, following inner inclinations toward good, and lolling around in God's presence.

If we have not practiced some of these relationship builders with God, discerning his voice and therefore our purpose becomes a discouraging if not insurmountable challenge. If such is the case, I recommend closing this book and focusing on the divine relationship before pursuing a destiny. It is this relationship that saves and preserves the soul, our vehicle for pursuing purpose. "Only in Christ will you find complete fulfillment. In Him you may be united to the Godhead in conscious, vital awareness," advised the thought-provoking preacher A. W. Tozer. "Remember that all of God is accessible to you through Christ. Cultivate His knowledge above everything else on earth."[6]

Cultivating this relationship also sharpens our awareness of other blocks to God's voice expressed to the woman within. These blocks could be personal sin, too much busyness, low self-esteem (thinking we are not worthy of hearing from God or that he can't use us for his purposes), or disbelief that he holds our life's road map. Not only can these blocks hinder us from discovering our purpose, but they also diffuse the effectiveness of that purpose when we're in the thick of fulfilling it.

For instance, for several years I'd felt a barrier in my soul. In my infrequent quiet moments I actually felt it lodged in my chest, and my hurried and uninspired attempts to pray it away didn't work. For the most part I kept so busy I couldn't attend to it seriously. Nor did I want to. I sensed this barrier blocked a closer walk with God, but I feared what I'd have to sacrifice to eradicate it. I didn't need any more pain or pressure in my life.

Then in the course of my work I accepted an assignment to propose a book of selections from another author's body of published work. On a Saturday afternoon I halfheartedly began skimming one of her books. A few pages in, though, I slowed down and read more carefully. Several hours later, still seated in a living room chair, I finished a straight-through reading of the book. It wasn't an extraordinary style but the message that gripped me.

This author candidly wrote of passing through a "dark night of the soul" and in later chapters listed the sins that separated her from God: presumption, hardness of heart, self-centeredness, self-pity, anger, and resentment.[7] I recognized these as my own sins and mentally added arrogance to the list. I admitted to God that while following my purpose, I'd slipped into these attitudes about my job and coworkers. Then I asked him to forgive me of each sin.

The process was simple. I flooded with relief, and ever since I've been free of that internal barrier. If a well-meaning human had pointed out these sins to me, because of the toll of constant busyness, I'd have interpreted the remarks as criticism, resisted the truth, and spun excuses for myself. But when I slowed down and tended to my soul, the Holy Spirit grabbed the opportunity to convict and cleanse me.

This episode reminded me of a guideline I learned from a wise woman years ago but had buried in a pileup of stress. When we hear the Holy Spirit's voice within, especially when it's a gentle voice of caution or correction, it leads to healing and freedom. If the voice condemns and brutalizes us, we can assume it's our unforgiving self or the unrelenting devil who dupes us into believing God wants to torture us. Listening to the Holy Spirit, who speaks to the woman within, is not something to fear if we're willing to trust and obey God. It is a comforting, liberating process that draws us closer to authenticating the unique woman he created each of us to be.

Authenticating Our Uniqueness

When with the Holy Spirit's influence we listen to and trust the woman within, when we're so hungry for authenticity that we confront what needs internal attention and correction, we open a channel for hearing and confirming our purpose. At the same time, pinpointing a purpose is not so ethereal that only the mystical and monastic can do it. Much of our purpose already resides within us; again, we only need to look honestly within and ask questions.

The key is truthfulness. We need to be true to ourselves by being truthful about ourselves. No holding back. No answers that reflect who we think we *should be* rather than who we *really are*. No worrying about what others will think.

Psychologist Marsha Sinetar, who has widely studied and written about authentic work, says that to be truthful about our real selves, our true purpose, we need to quell the fear of rejection. I believe this is particularly true for women. Traditionally we spend so much time assuring other people's happiness that we submerge ourselves. Christian women especially struggle with this submersion; somehow we think being true to ourselves is selfish and unspiritual—a betrayal of the people we love and our responsibilities to them. We worry that they will disapprove and abandon us, or at least make our lives miserable.

"Our need for love and belonging can be so strong that it blinds us to our most valuable talents and qualities," writes Sinetar. "We then live a life of pretense.... Some people have censored so much of themselves for so long that they forget what it is they do feel and think. They have consistently turned to others to gain love, acceptance, and safety. In adulthood, when they need to be authentic, they cannot recall how. They have not developed the requisite skills for distinctiveness. As a result, they are less than they would be—bland shells of what they were meant to be."[8]

However, when we choose truthfulness and authenticity, eventually the reverse of rejection happens to us. The more we become our God-intended selves, our real and creative selves, the more people we attract. Personal authenticity exudes a centeredness and peacefulness, a comfortableness with ourselves, to which others migrate. We are fully alive, wholly involved, internally motivated. We can serve others without devaluing ourselves. And we're certainly not bland.

One of my favorite "unbland" women has just finished graduate school. On the front of an invitation to celebrate Patty's graduation, a friend of hers printed this quotation:

The most visible creators I know of
are those artists whose
medium is life itself.
The ones who express
the inexpressible—without brush,
hammer, clay or guitar.
They neither paint nor sculpt—
their medium is being.
Whatever their presence touches
has increased life.
They see and don't have to draw,
they are the artists of being alive.[9]

While this poem defines my friend Patty, it could describe anyone who searches for and becomes the woman she's designed to be.
When we are doing what we love, we are also being someone who is
lovable. And once we choose to be truthful and authentic and artists of
being alive, the questions are so basic they could surprise us because we
probably already know bits of the answers.

What are my talents? What are my dreams? What is my calling?
Answered individually, these questions provide insight; melded together
and confirmed by God, they ignite purpose, pleasure, and passion. Yes,
pleasure and passion. Contrary to hedonistic or puritanical viewpoints,
these are the holy results of living authentically, of staying true to the
woman within and flowing in God's uniquely designed purpose. Christ

promises us an abundant life, and when we pursue the truth about our-selves, the truth sets us free to enjoy living.[10] But it is not for our pleasure only. In the movie *Chariots of Fire,* the track star Eric Liddell confided that when he ran, he felt God's pleasure.[11]

Assessing Our Talents

What are my talents? When a woman protests this question and says, "But I have no talents," I can almost hear the cosmic *Whack!* of her slapping God's face. How it must grieve him to hear this. After lov-ingly creating each of us as unique individuals, after molding us in his image of giftedness, we reject his spectacular handiwork. Maybe this is a misunderstanding of talents, but more likely it is self-pity. When we utter "I have no talents," we beg for someone to bolster our shaky self-image.

Everyone possesses talents. Some people received more talents than we did; some talents garner more public recognition than others. To jealously compare ourselves with others and mourn our "lesser" or "nonexistent" talents shoves away the satisfaction of fulfilling our own purpose. Besides, the "who gets what" decisions belong to God; our responsibility is to exercise the talents he gave us.

Christ emphasized this stewardship in the parable of the talents. In this story as a nobleman prepared for a trip, he gathered his servants and gave them talents of money, each according to his ability. (A talent equaled about a thousand dollars.) After the master left, the man with five talents immediately set about to earn five more talents. The servant who received two talents earned two more, but the one who possessed one talent buried it in the ground.

When the nobleman returned, he sent for his servants and inquired about the talents. "The man who had received the five talents brought the other five. 'Master,' he said, 'you entrusted me with five talents. See, I have gained five more.'

"His master replied, 'Well done, good and faithful servant! You have been faithful with a few things; I will put you in charge of many things. Come and share your master's happiness!'"

This scenario repeated itself for the servant who multiplied his two talents into four.

But the man who received one talent didn't fare well. "'Master,' he said, 'I...was afraid and went out and hid your talent in the ground. See, here is what belongs to you.'

"His master replied, 'You wicked, lazy servant!... you should have put my money on deposit with the bankers, so that when I returned I would have received it back with interest.

"'Take the talent from him and give it to the one who has the ten talents. For everyone who has will be given more, and he will have an abundance. Whoever does not have, even what he has will be taken from him.'"[12]

Although this parable speaks of money, it serves as a metaphor for the use of our God-endowed abilities. In fact, this "use it or lose it" principle occurs repeatedly in life. To name a few, exercising, investing, networking, performing, and gardening require constant attention or else we lose the ground we've gained. God takes seriously the endowment and use of his gifts to us.

In addition to our innate talents, God endows spiritual gifts when he fills us with the Holy Spirit. These gifts, which are manifestations of the Spirit and supernatural in nature, may enhance our innate talents with a spiritual anointing (administration, teaching, giving) or add to our repertoire of abilities (faith, healing, knowledge, wisdom).[13] Often Christians receive a cluster of spiritual gifts rather than just one, but the Holy Spirit determines these allotments, not us.

Whatever spiritual gifts we receive, God expects us to use them for the good of his children. And when we assess both our talents and spiritual gifting, we're only steps away from defining our purpose.

If we still have trouble thinking of ourselves as talented or spiritually gifted, we can ask ourselves, "What am I good at doing?" These are the things physical (working with numbers or coordinating colors and fabrics) or relational (encouraging people in their marriages or helping them heal wounds) or spiritual (communicating great truths or praying for miracles) that we do well and the work satisfies us. They include things we do now and things we stopped doing somewhere along the path to today.

Richard Bolles claims that God has already revealed our purpose to us by "writing it in our members" or our personal makeup. "We are to begin deciphering our unique Mission by studying our talents and skills, and more particularly which ones (or One) we most rejoice to use."[14] The ones that emerge may surprise us because they have been so long forgotten, or they may scare us because they require that we instigate change, but please resist the urge to squelch them. Searching for purpose is daring to dream.

Dancing Our Dreams

What are my dreams? Disregarding real or imaginary constraints, how would we like to use our talents? What desires are tucked in the heart? What would we love to spend a lifetime doing? What would bring joy and meaning and contentment? What accomplishment stays buried for fear we're incapable of achieving it or that somebody might laugh at the idea? Risk pulling it out and mulling it over. God gives us the desires of our hearts.[15] Could it be we've repressed a dream that is actually his purpose for us?

God-inspired dreams blend both the realistic and the impossible. They are obtainable enough that we can imagine ourselves, with our innate though inexperienced talents, pursuing them. They are impossible enough that we need God's power and intervention to reach them.

As a chubby girl I danced about in my parents' driveway, dressed in a crinoline slip, pretending to be a ballerina (much to the horror of my mother, who believed a young lady should never appear outdoors in an undergarment). The dancing evoked joy (at least within me), but it didn't point to my purpose. The same was true for the dramas I staged in the garage. I didn't possess the innate abilities or internal commitment to be a dancer or an actor, and even at a young age I sensed this. But when I wrote in my diary, "I want to write a book," something inside said, "Yes, the impossible is possible." I could be an author.

"Author" fit my natural talents and inclinations. Without prompting from anyone I spent hours in my bedroom, reading, daydreaming, writing poetry, and making up stories in my head. Years later I learned that I descended from a line of writers on the maternal side of my family tree and observed with fascination as my ten-year-old niece, also without coaxing, stayed up late to fill spiral notebooks with her original novels. For my niece and me, purpose resided in a genetic heritage and introduced itself in our childhood imaginations. I still love dance and the theater, but I've never regretted my choice to become a writer. The working out of that choice, though, has continually necessitated God's guidance and willingness to create minor miracles. With his help I can dance a dream that suits who I am.

For most of us, childhood is a reliable place to revisit when looking for lost dreams. It is an innocent time when we're closely aligned with whom God created us to be—before fear, stress, expectations, and responsibilities choke our courage and creativity. As mothers, we can encourage our children to stay true to these inclinations and pray that their playfulness bursts into God's purpose for them. My mother, certain within herself that I'd be an author, quietly prayed me through my turbulent twenties when I didn't want to be a Christian or a writer. And I am grateful.

Considering Our Calling

What is my calling? To answer this question, we consider not only what we do, but whom we're to serve with our talents and dreams. My favorite explanation of calling originated with novelist Frederick Buechner: "The place God calls you to is the place where your deep gladness and the world's deep hunger meet."[16] God doesn't give us talents and spiritual gifts just to lavish them on ourselves. He expects us to use them for his service, and his kingdom focuses on redeeming people.

Frequently a calling falls in step with the natural course of our lives; other times, it radically uproots us from familiar surroundings. A calling can last a lifetime; it can last for only a specified time period. The direction and duration depend on God's desire for each individual, so it's vital to ask him periodically to reaffirm our calling and amend it with his delightful detours.

However, I do not believe that calling, though it stretches our talents and challenges our priorities, falls outside of our desires and giftedness. Calling dwells within our overall purpose. A woman who defines her purpose as "pointing people to God" may engage in social work in her twenties, raise a family and sponsor support groups in her thirties and forties, and for the rest of her life travel the globe as a conference speaker. In each of these seasonal callings she points people to God.

Wherever we land, we can practice our purpose if we're open to the possibilities and insist on authenticity by listening to the woman within. To say, "I am just a homemaker" or "I am just a salesclerk" or a college student or retiree or any other role in life is shortsighted. Granted, there are times when roles and responsibilities diminish the amount of time we give to our purpose, but if the mission reflects our innate design, there are always at least small ways in which we can express it.

We're misdirected, too, when we think, "If I really want to do it, it must not be God's way for me." Unless we're chasing after sin, a deep desire most likely indicates a purpose-filled direction. Unfortunately a certain brand of preaching (hopefully outdated by now) leads people to believe that God calls us to what we hate so we can endlessly toil and suffer. True, we can't escape hard work and pain to achieve in life, but it's far different to struggle and sacrifice for something we love than for something we feel stuck with.

Marsha Sinetar suggests that to find an enduring life purpose we can ask ourselves, "What's worth doing?" "What attracts me?" "What makes me willing to stretch and struggle?"[17] I would add to these, "What stirs my passion?" When we suffer within a passionate purpose, we can still sing, "It is well with my soul."[18]

Defining the Passion

When we've answered the questions and striven to stay true to the woman within, we can then prayerfully define our purpose. Many ways exist to structure a purpose statement, but I recommend describing it in terms general enough to span a lifetime but specific enough to guide our goal and decision making. It can also state the people we want to reach and the desired outcome of serving them.

For example, when I add in the audience to whom I'm called during this life stage and the desired results of exercising my talents, my purpose is "to publish the glad tidings to women, encouraging them to become all God created them to be." Here are other examples of stated purposes:

- *To compose music that nurtures the soul.*
- *To help people eat healthily, freeing them to live as God's temples.*
- *To assist the Holy Spirit in healing children's wounded hearts so they can grow into whole and spiritually alive adults.*
- *To train believers to make a difference for God in the world.*
- *To manage finances so families and companies align with biblical principles about money.*
- *To intercede in prayer for downtrodden people around the globe so their physical and spiritual needs are met.*

If at this juncture we're still uncertain about our inner selves, it is better at least to experiment with a stated purpose than to continue an ineffectual, meandering lifestyle. God honors faith, and we can ask him to "establish the work of our hands"[19] when it feels as though we're bumbling along. It is he who directs our steps and keeps us on course.

We can be assured that the "steps of a [good] man are directed and established by the Lord, when he delights in his way [and He busies Himself with his every step]. Though he falls, he shall not be utterly cast down, for the Lord grasps his hand in support and upholds him."[20]

It is this hand of support that leads us forward into a personal vision.

Chapter Four

Vision

Seeing and Believing the Unseen

To believe in something not yet proved
and to underwrite it with our lives:
it is the only way we can leave the future open.

LILLIAN SMITH

FOR MOMENTS I stand still in the meadow, wondering where its gentle breezes will nudge me next. I've come to the French countryside to wander, to adore the summertime and its glories, to shake off the din of too much living.

And during this pause I hear music.

I strain for the flute's melody—as faint as the wisps of wind— and follow it. Quickening my pace, I hear the notes grow stronger, more lyrical. Then cresting a small hill I spot two peasant-dressed, barefooted girls huddled in a valley below, the older one creating music beyond her years and the younger leaning in close and intently observing.

I stop suddenly but quietly so they cannot detect me. And just as quickly I grow entranced by the Shakespearean quality of this setting. It seems as though any second now Puck and his companions will appear, scattering fairy dust and making merry mischief.[1] I long to join them, casting away responsibility and pretending nothing matters but this magical interlude.

But then I turn my head, and much too soon I'm back to brushing my teeth.

I'm not really in France; I'm standing in my bathroom, looking at a print that hangs on the wall above an oak bureau. It's a copy of the work *Two Girls* by the French painter Adolph William Bouguereau. He completed the painting in 1900, but for me it is not a dated depiction; it is contemporary and real.

As I ready for the day, I sometimes envision myself in the French countryside, feeling just as delighted to discover these young girls as when I first happened upon the original painting in a Denver art museum. Rounding the corner of an exhibition room, I spotted the sizable yet delicate canvas and sucked in my breath. *How beautiful, how very beautiful,* I thought and called a friend to my side to appreciate it with me. Later that day she bought me a print of the painting for my birthday, and that's how a French theme entered my downstairs bathroom.

Several years later another friend gave me a small painting from Paris which I hung near the bathtub. A few soaps from Provence, some French-inspired towels and window scarves, and voilà, I am transported to a European country. (I have a good imagination.)

Actually I've never traveled to France, but encountering the golden-framed girls and their flute, I imagine myself there. I can see myself in a country inn or a Parisian bistro, and I know that someday I will visit the land of the Louvre and flirty waiters named Pierre. Who knows? I might even find that meadow, some girls, and a flute. Whatever the case, I *will* explore France. For this, I have vision.

The Necessity of Vision

Do my bathroom musings about France seem silly and far-fetched?

Welcome to the world of vision. In this realm one woman's dream is another woman's foolishness. The satirist Jonathan Swift said, "Vision is the art of seeing things invisible"[2] and some of history's greatest visionaries have been mistaken for lunatics instead of artists and saints. Yet the Bible says that without a vision, people perish.[3] Vision— imagining what can be—keeps us physically and spiritually alive.

Daily most of us function as visionaries in the physical arena. Rising in the morning, we think about what we'll do and who we'll meet; we plan meals and consider the stacks of work before us; we plot appointments and contemplate garden beds, even if we envision these events only moments before accomplishing them. For the most part we

naturally fill our roles as pragmatic, physical visionaries. Out of neces-
sity we "see" tasks in our heads because we need to get things done.

Without these daily visions society would turn chaotic (or at least
more so than now) or shut down. On a smaller scale, we'd miss out on
the wonderful encounters of life: hobbies, family time, friendships,
delicious food, church activities, a home that's worth coming home to.
However, many people never move beyond this level of vision. They
see ahead only far enough to live comfortably or, in more stressful
cases, just to eke by.

Certainly in war- and famine-devastated countries, people push
just to exist. How can they cull out internal dreams when circumstances
funnel toward one goal: merely to stay alive? Their limited vision is
understandable. In basic marketing, education, and psychology courses,
students study psychologist Abraham Maslow's hierarchy, a triangular-
shaped diagram that visually explains the origins of human
motivation.4 At the base of the triangle sit our basic physiological
needs such as food, water, and rest. If these needs stay unmet, people
usually don't progress to the higher levels of motivation: safety, love,
esteem, and self-actualization. They freeze frame on meeting biologi-
cal demands.

For most of us, though, the life-preserving needs get met. After
losing a job, when confronting an illness or solving a family crisis, we
may justifiably dip into a survival mode. But for the most part we live
with—and often well above—the essentials. Yet we can miss *catching*

sight of who we can be and how we can make a difference for God. We lack spiritual vision.

Spiritual vision believes in the possibilities for pursuing our purpose, motivating us to meet our greatest potential by accomplishing God's work in the world. Spiritual vision propels the practical outworking of our purpose, encouraging us to act upon what we know. At the same time, spiritual vision is "the stuff that dreams are made of,"[5] but usually we don't dream expansively enough about how to fulfill our purpose. We may even know something is missing within us but be unable to identify it as a lack of spiritual vision.

The poetic allegory of Christ's death and resurrection, *The Singer,* exposes the reason for this predicament.

"Hello, Singer," said the voice he knew too well. "Welcome to the quiet of the grove. Does the senseless empty crowd offend you?"

The Singer's only offense came in knowing that the World Hater always seemed to know what he was thinking.

"How did you manage to make them cherish all this nothingness?" he asked the World Hater.

"I simply make them feel embarrassed to admit that they are incomplete. A man would rather close his eyes than see himself as your Father-Spirit does. I teach them to exalt their emptiness and thus preserve the dignity of man."

"They need the dignity of God."

"You tell them that. I sell a cheaper product."[6]

The World Hater had one thing right. Living fully—living with spiritual vision—is costly. But it's also passionate, exhilarating, surprising, and enduring. And it births when we offer our emptiness to God.

Filling Up with Vision

The Bible speaks of God filling up the people who walk with him and leaving empty those who don't.[7] When we repentingly accept his grace and forgiveness, God fills our spirit with his, but that is only the beginning.

Paul wrote to the church at Ephesus about the overflowing abundance available to the followers of God through Jesus Christ. "I pray that out of his glorious riches he [God] may strengthen you with power through his Spirit in your inner being," he began. "And I pray that you, being rooted and established in love, may have power, together with all the saints, to grasp how wide and long and high and deep is the love of Christ, and to know this love that surpasses knowledge— *that you may be filled to the measure of all the fullness of God.*"

Then, as if this isn't enough, the apostle adds a frequently recited benediction: "Now to him who is able to do *immeasurably more than all we ask or imagine,* according to his power that is at work within us, to him be glory...throughout all generations."[8]

Not only does God give us his Holy Spirit, he affords us inner power and strength. Not only does he lavish us with immeasurable love, he fills us with everything available in himself and from his resources. Not only does he answer our requests, he exceeds our expectations. And this is the essence of spiritual vision: God filling us with himself and then playing a game of one-upmanship on our dreams. He longs to fulfill our purpose in breathtaking ways we don't even imagine. So when we live without spiritual vision, we are blocking God from his desires; he is not depriving us of ours. It is us not making good on our life purpose.

The Father-Creator wants to fill us with vision, and if we understand and trust his good ways, this vision will captivate and motivate us through the seasons of its development. A God-endowed vision is a not-yet-realized goal we feel honored to pursue, for it wraps together our talents, dreams, calling, personality—our very soul—and ignites our purpose. But be warned: as with accepting God's salvation, a vision requires giving all of ourselves, and perhaps this is why people don't follow their dreams. They're in the habit of hiding and holding back parts of themselves. But our God is a consuming fire.9 Embarking on his adventure requires that we grow, change, and improve along with it, discarding what hinders effectiveness and accepting new ways of being.

In her book about faith and art Madeleine L'Engle explains, "We have to be braver than we think we can be, because God is constantly calling us to be more than we are, to see through plastic sham to living, breathing reality, and to break down our defenses of self-protection in order to be free to receive and give love. With God, even a rich man can enter the narrow gate to heaven. Earthbound as we are, even we can walk on water."[10]

God wants to break down our defenses—whatever might block our vision—so we can receive his love and offer it to others. His end goal is the redemption of people, and with this objective in mind we can revel in our resulting defenselessness. It is the open, willing heart that God fills with vision and uses in his service.

Feeling and Facing Fear

Twice a month I attend the meetings of several women entrepreneurs who gather to brainstorm marketing ideas for their businesses. While we call ourselves the Entrepreneurial Marketing Group (EMG), we're not as accomplished and courageous as the title sounds. We each own a sole proprietorship and need encouragement to survive the unpredictability of a business start-up. We've laughed about calling ourselves the CEOs and presidents of our one-woman, home-based companies, admitting that a big title and a business card can make anyone appear successful.

As I've listened to this apologetic laughter and the discussions, it's struck me that women can be their own worst enemies regarding vision. Even if we want to believe in something bigger for ourselves— something beyond today that fulfills our desires—we frequently erect barriers toward it. At each EMG meeting we target one member's business and help her solve marketing dilemmas, but as the suggestions roll in, often the featured woman's first impulse is to say, "I can't do that." The rest of the group can think of various ways she could, but the woman can't see it. An unseen barrier blocks her imagination.

In fact, despite our society's strides of the last thirty years, I've observed this tendency in every women's group I've associated with closely. Almost automatically we offer reasons why we're not worthy, capable, or available to tackle what's new and challenging. In some cases when questioned about our reasons, we can't even explain why we can't. We just think we can't.

This resistance keeps women from seeking, finding, and enjoying vision. It can express itself in various attitudes and behaviors, suggested below. As I created this list, the ideas flowed easily because through the years I've constructed most of these barriers myself.

Besetting sin	Lack of finances
Busyness	Laziness
Competitiveness	Low self-esteem
Disbelief	People's opinions
Emotional wounds	Resentment
Fear of failure	Self-pity
Fear of success	Social standing
Health limitations	Pride
Jealousy	Worry
Lack of discipline	Wrong location

Probably we all can find our excuses on this list, plus add a few unusual barriers of our own. But what creates the resistance? Mostly it's fear. We fear what vision will cost us in time, money, energy, sacrifice, preparation, security, and reputation. If we step into a vision, we could feel unprepared for the challenge and defenseless against the unknown. Most of us want security, and if it weren't for God whispering "There's more" and stirring up a restlessness within us, we'd probably stay put. We prefer familiarity over risk.

But clinging to this preference misses God's best for us. He designed us to be purposeful, granting us the capacity to grow socially, emotionally, spiritually, and intellectually throughout our lives. Jesus never taught us to be comfortable and maintain the status quo. He commanded us to go, grow, and change the world. Inertia is our choice.

I'm not suggesting that when we embrace a vision, we never feel afraid. I'm recommending that instead of saying "I can't," we declare, "I can't by myself, but with God's help, I can." This statement offers our fear to God and confesses our willingness to move forward by faith, despite our misgivings. It also allows God to begin the miracle of changing us and fulfilling the vision. Because he granted us the freedom to choose, God needs our willingness to start the process, but that's all. He takes over from there. Though fearful, we can comfort ourselves with the fact that God fulfills his promises; he makes good on the visions he plants in his children's anxious hearts.

Believe me, I know about anxiety. I can't think of any major goal or change in my life that hasn't filled me with fear. It is my Achilles' heel, the jugular vein that Satan grabs first when he wants me to abandon a vision and turn back. I've lain in my bed at night so riddled with fear I thought I'd be too paralyzed to lift myself up in the morning. I've spent weekends locked in my house, crying and sometimes crumpled in a corner or sprawled on the floor because of the overwhelming anxiety. I've feared what people might think of me if I took a risk and, worse yet, what I might think of myself. I've even feared the fear.

Through these experiences, though, I've grown to depend on God's faithfulness and his ability to banish fear. Once during a church service, as I sat slumped in a pew and filled with worry, the pastor announced, "Nothing can keep God from fulfilling his purpose for your life." It's the only line I remember from that sermon and initially I didn't believe it. I thought a vision depended upon me, that being afraid meant my dreams couldn't materialize. Since then I've learned that human fear can't bar God from accomplishing his will on the earth and in us. He listens to and destroys our fears because he loves us without limit and chooses to engage us in his work. He wants us free from internal and vision-blocking barriers.

I've also learned that fear hits hardest when we're isolated. We need the prayers and support of an extended spiritual family to help ward off or exorcise our fears. I've realized that while I can effectively engage in spiritual warfare to demolish another person's fear, I cannot accomplish this for myself. I need another believer—and sometimes several intercessors—to lay hands on me and pray against the fear until it flees. I've also assembled a group of spiritually attuned friends who form an ongoing prayer team dedicated to my needs and requests. They believe in and support the outworking of my purpose and vision. I've also sought biblical counseling and sound medical advice to help eradicate my fears, and I recommend the same to anyone gripped by anxiety, but not to the exclusion of communication with God.

With God's power and a spiritual family's support, we need not succumb to fear or any of its barriers. In the best sense of the word, God wants us defenseless—dependent upon his resources and open to his leading.

Seeking and Finding Vision

When we open ourselves to vision, we can think of it as narrowing down or further clarifying our life purpose. A vision tells us the specific work we're to accomplish and the particular subgroup of people we're to reach. In addition, the duration of a vision can vary. We may pursue one vision for a lifetime, or over a lifetime God may ask us to pursue several. A woman's purpose may be to present the gospel to children, and within that framework she follows a vision to develop Sunday school classes for urban grade-school children. At another time God may call her to volunteer at a year-round camp for single-parent kids or to work with the junior high group. Same purpose, different vision.

True to his creative nature, God fills people with spiritual vision in a myriad of ways, using methods that fit the individuals and circumstances involved and ranging anywhere from the dramatic confrontation to a quiet knowing within.

In the Bible we read stories in which the Lord imparted vision through dramatic means. In the Old Testament, God used an apocalyptic visitation, complete with a windstorm and four part-man, part-angelic creatures to send the prophet Ezekiel to the rebellious Israelites. In the New Testament, the angel Gabriel announced to the virgin Mary her pregnancy. And Saul, the Jewish persecutor of Christians, was struck blind by a light and told he'd carry the gospel to the Gentiles.[11]

These announcements were exotic measures for unusual tasks, but God still uses creative ways to get our attention. In my own spiritual quest God once spoke to me about which women I should reach for a particular project. During a late afternoon nap I dreamed I was lying on my stomach while a woman I recognized cleaned my feet. I'd gone to junior high with Karen, who attended church but didn't live as a Christian.

In the dream Karen showed me the heels of my feet: each one had a hole bored into it. When I peered into the holes, it horrified me to observe layers of crusty, dead skin instead of vibrant flesh and blood.

"You should let the physician take care of your feet," remarked Karen, and then I woke up.

Lying on the couch, I mentally reviewed the dream. It disturbed me. I knew it meant something, but I didn't know how to interpret it. Wanting clues, I grabbed my Bible and looked up verses that mentioned feet. This one stood out to me: "How beautiful on the mountains are the feet of those who bring good news, who proclaim peace, who bring good tidings, who proclaim salvation, who say to Zion, 'Your God reigns!'"[12]

The feet carry God's good news, I thought.

Then the telephone rang. When I told my friend on the line about the dream and the verse, she asked, "Judy, is there anything in your life that would bar you from reaching women? Anything that would keep you from taking the good news to women like Karen?"

I began to cry. "Yes," I said softly. "There's a specific sin in my life that I need to take care of."

We talked awhile longer, and after I hung up the phone, it all fell together. Karen represented the women God was calling me to reach, but I could not effectively carry the good news to them with this sin in my life. I needed to let Christ, the Great Physician, abolish my sin and prepare my feet for ministry.

This is the most mystical way God has spoken to me about out-reach, and though I dream every night, something about the quality of that dream and its immediate confirmations prompted me to listen. However, I don't recommend assuming that every or even most of our dreams are visions from God. Sometimes our dreams result from watching movies before going to bed, so as a caution we can ask God to confirm and reconfirm whether a message is from him. In my case this interpretation also withstood the test of time.

For the most part I've followed a vision through promises from the Bible, the intersection of circumstances, "coincidental" messages and confirmations from others, and a strong inner tug. Still, God's ways of leading me are not the measuring sticks for how others hear from him. As I mentioned earlier, God speaks to individuals in individual ways. There are people who've prayed, searched the Bible, listed the possibilities, and did what most appealed to them—and have faithfully carried out a vision. (To their credit, these people seem more spiritually malleable than I am. I can be so strong-willed that I need a direct wallop from God to get my attention.)

Frequently a vision births from our particular life experiences. When the doctors sent Anne Frähm home from the hospital to die, she searched for ways to heal the cancer eating away her body. By adopting a healthy lifestyle through organic foods, vitamin supplements, and exercise, she reversed her death sentence and now lives cancer-free. In turn, Anne helps others avoid or heal illness through her ministry, HealthQuarters. Likewise, some recovering alcoholics help addicts free themselves from drugs and alcohol. Mothers of disabled children form support groups for families in similar situations. I know of a woman who, based on her training and experience in drama, conducts an informal ministry to actors in New York. When sparking vision, God specializes in diversity.

But there is one characteristic that with a few exceptions everyday visionaries share. They actively seek God's will. I keep a tattered old book in my library to remind myself of this. It's titled *By Searching*, written by Isobel Kuhn. As a teenager I read this small paperback about a college student whom God called to missionary work in

China. Isobel did not discover God's vision all at once; she searched for it while keeping up with her school and work schedule.

In retrospect Isobel laid out this truth: God asks us to search for him and his answers, and if we seek, we will find them. She offered these Scriptures and her story as evidence.

The question: Canst thou by searching find out God?—Job 11:7

❧ *The answer: Ye shall seek me, and find me, when ye shall search for me with all your heart.—Jeremiah 29:13*

❧ *Jesus said unto him, I am the way, the truth, and the life; no man cometh unto the Father, but by me.—John 14:6*

❧ *Search the Scriptures... they are they which testify of me.— John 5:39*

❧ *If any man will do his will, he shall know of the doctrine, whether it be of God.—John 7:17*

❧ *He is a rewarder of them that diligently seek him.— Hebrews 11:6.*[13]

By searching we can find the vision we're to follow. However, as we search, we're not to use a secular barometer that measures showmanship, big productions, and high visibility as what's best. We're to listen for what God has prepared for us, within the abilities, personality, and circumstances that constitute our purpose. In his upsidedown kingdom, the small and humble outreaches can deserve the most praise.[14] What matters is that we find our vision and follow it wholeheartedly. Whether we're the neighborhood mom to latch-key children or the owner of an international operation or a volunteer at a nursing home, we're to do it "as working for the Lord,"[15] and therein we discover satisfaction. With God, it is not prestige that counts but the condition of a heart.

A New Way of Seeing

We can confirm a specific vision in the same manner Hannah Whithall Smith taught us to listen for God's voice: through the harmony of Scripture, circumstances, convictions of our higher judgment, and inward impressions of the Holy Spirit.

For me, the Spirit's inward nudge has grown particularly strong on occasion. Sometimes it's felt more like a powerful compulsion instead of a nudge, as if without my speaking, it would burst out of my mouth. During times of discouragement and no visible fruition in sight, this inner compulsion has sprung up and kept me believing that a vision was from God. To recognize this compulsion as from him, though, I had to learn to see with the eyes of my spirit instead of fixating on external circumstances. Spiritual vision requires that we cultivate a new way of seeing.

In the delightful novel *Portofino,* ten-year-old Calvin, the son of fundamentalist missionaries, travels with his parents and sisters to Italy for a summer vacation. In the small resort town Calvin befriends Gino, a whiskey-drinking painter who pontificates on art and life. Calvin tells us about Gino's belief that "knowing how to look" is the secret to creating masterpieces.

I left my T-shirt and sandals on the rocks and dove in and swam underwater as far as I could, then turned over and swam on my back almost the whole way to the beach. I stared up at the little clouds in the pale blue August sky and wondered why sky and clouds looked so different from one place to the next. This was an Italian sky for sure. You'd never see the sky looking like this in Switzerland or England.

Gino said that the English never produced any truly great painters because they didn't have good light. Italy had the best light, he said, and that was why they had the greatest painters. I had asked Gino, "What about Holland and Rembrandt and all?" and Gino said, "Eet ees all tooa small! All too interior! Portraits yes, families seetting at table, yes, but Botticelli? Never! 'Ow could Venus be born out of the gray Northa Sea in a rainstorm on a colda day?!" And he would turn back to his easel and say, "No, no, Italia ees where you musta paint! Painta Life! Germany for cars and beer, America for preetty girls and beesiness, but Italia ees where you paint!"

It was true. The light was different in Italy. It made things glow.

Janet [Calvin's sister] said that was just my imagination and light was light wherever it was but she was wrong. When I told Gino what she had said, he said, "That'sa why 'alf the world cannot understanda art, they don'ta know 'ow to look!"[16]

When pursuing a specific vision within our purpose, knowing how to look can make all of the difference. Not only to find the vision, but also to carry it out. For when we catch sight of God's vision for us, it doesn't culminate immediately. God's vision is for an appointed time,[17] and the preparation can last for years. Consequently, we keep looking ahead, believing in our future influence while fully participating in today.

For this, we need focus.

Chapter Five

Focus

Pursuing What Matters the Most

❧

How we spend our days is, of course,
how we spend our lives....
There is no shortage of good days.
It is good lives that are hard to come by.

ANNIE DILLARD

CLARE BOOTHE LUCE grabbed for everything she could squeeze out of life and its accomplishments. Born in the tenements, at an early age Clare vowed to abandon obscurity and become memorable through her work and associations.

That she did. In the 1930s she rose to managing editor of *Vanity Fair.* Through her later marriage to Henry Luce, she influenced the man who created the TIME, INC. publishing empire. Together they grew powerfully rich. But for Clare that wasn't enough. After stints in magazine publishing she also wrote much-acclaimed plays, served two terms in Congress, and became the United States ambassador to Italy. Clare's accomplishments labeled her "a woman ahead of her time," and to top it off, she fashionably displayed her beautiful face and figure.

To the public, there was nothing Clare couldn't do, nothing she didn't own. In private, her friends and family observed that she relentlessly pursued what she never achieved: inner peace and satisfaction. Clare competed against Henry for fame and resented his control over the business. She ignored her daughter and collected enemies almost as fast as she engaged in love affairs with intelligent men. She suffered paranoid depressions and thwarted Henry's attempts at divorce when their marriage shriveled.

For Clare, doing and possessing more than anyone else was never enough. "One achieves so much less than one's expectations," she said toward the end of her life. "I was thinking at one time of writing my memoirs and calling it, 'Confessions of an Unsuccessful Woman.' I've done too many things and it all doesn't stack up."[1]

Compare Clare's story to Evelyn Harris Brand's life.

Evelyn enjoyed ribbon-and-lace comfort as the daughter of a prosperous, turn-of-the-century London merchant. Then at thirty she heard about the great physical and spiritual needs in India and committed herself to serve there. In that country she married Jesse Brand, a handsome visionary who shared her passion for the poor mountain people. The couple set up housekeeping in "the mountains of death" and pursued their vision.

Nothing about their chosen work came easily. The monstrous terrain fought back as they worked and traveled it. Bound in a tight caste system, the people worshiped devils and feared a witch doctor who blocked medically trained Jesse from tending the sick. Yet in spite of setbacks he and Evelyn applied their resourcefulness and determination to the hopeless looking situation. They were naturally gifted for this calling and worked building homes, schools, and dispensaries; teaching trades and hygiene; introducing agricultural products and techniques; and preaching to surrounding communities. Yet it was years before anyone responded to their life-changing claims about Christ.

Determined to stick with it, Jesse gradually increased his preaching jaunts to over ninety hamlets. After the Brands' two children, Paul and Connie, left for school in America, Evelyn sometimes accompanied her husband on these trips. Through the years she had nurtured her talent as a landscape painter, and during one train journey Jesse wrote to the kids, "Mother nearly frantic because she could not paint both sides at once." Though surrounded by hardship, life together was good.

Evelyn's dream of marital togetherness didn't last for a lifetime though. After a trip to South India, Jesse came down with a high fever and four days later, at age forty-four, died from blackwater fever. When the mission board expected Evelyn then to leave the hills, she refused. The Brands had committed to reaching all five mountain ranges, and if they couldn't minister together, Evelyn would go alone. Her antidote for grief was continuing the work Jesse loved.

So Evelyn stayed on. At retirement age she quit the mission board and moved to yet another mountain, supported by a family inheritance. "It's terribly marvelous to be used by God," she wrote. And used she was. "Granny Brand" served in the hills another thirty years before she died there at age ninety-five.[2]

This One Thing I Do

Even though I read about Clare and Evelyn several years ago, I'm still affected by their contrasting attitudes at the end of their lives. While Clare lived glamorously and broadly, she died bitter and alone. Evelyn, though poor and not widely traveled, finished her life satisfied and triumphant. Aside from their obvious spiritual differences, Evelyn mastered an element of success that Clare never did: the ability to focus. Clare jumped restlessly from interest to interest; Evelyn unflinchingly pursued one goal. Their contrasting conclusions present a lesson for anyone interested in purpose-filled living, for purpose without focus stacks up to no purpose at all.

Focus is "to fix or settle on one thing; [to] concentrate"[3] on it to the exclusion of other interests, no matter how worthy, intriguing, and rewarding those pursuits might be. Focus requires that we funnel our energy into one overarching purpose, one compelling vision—if not one a lifetime, at least one at a time. Focus separates the excellent from the mediocre, the noteworthy from the inconsequential, the fulfilled from the restless. Focus makes our God-given dreams come true and is among the most arduous and rewarding life choices we'll ever face.

However, if we've chosen our purpose well—a purpose that wells from the soul and spills over with passion—focus becomes the logical next step. The young Georgia O'Keeffe, stretching to find her voice as a painter, personified focus. One of Georgia's biographers wrote of her stint as an art teacher in Texas: "She painted on days when she didn't teach and between classes on other days—continually, prolifically, spontaneously, urgently, with growing excitement and sureness. As she invented a way to express her intense feelings, she reduced her pictures to a few simple, straightforward shapes and colors, much like the uncluttered landscape itself, and much the way her Mexican pupils in Amarillo had painted—and her own style began to emerge."[1]

Georgia's artistic style—straightforward and uncluttered—also describes any woman who designs a life of purpose. As we fall more in love with our purpose, we willingly ferret out the distractions, the unnecessary elements that diffuse our energy, attention, and ability to reach a purposeful goal. We grow attuned to the Holy Spirit within, hearing a melody composed just for us and hushing the cacophony without. We claim, "This one thing I do" and do it gladly, letting much of the world pass by at a distance.

This is not to say focus emerges without struggle. In fact, focus usually births itself through the painful pruning of our lives. And if we possess various interests and abilities (as most of us do), we repeatedly weather the frustration of choosing the best over the good. For example, I imagine myself earning a good living as an interior decorator, a flower gardener, or a gourmet cook, if I chose to change my life purpose. These creative endeavors nurture my soul, and they're easier for me than writing, but I can't let them overtake God's calling to me as a writer and editor.

This is never so frustrating as when a publishing deadline hits in the spring or summertime. Neither the planting nor the publishing season waits for anyone, and I'm constantly torn between digging in the dirt and pounding on the computer. I also long to devote hours to decorating the house and entertaining friends, so I must constantly relegate these interests to hobbies that don't overtake my main purpose. Or sometimes I let them lie dormant when working on a big project.

I realize these choices don't sound that difficult, but other decisions to focus have nearly torn my heart in half: moving to another state, leaving behind extended family, and deciding, out of obedience to God's desire, not to marry during these developmental years of my purpose. Through these decisions, I am intimate with both tears and loneliness, assurance and fulfillment.

Passion Versus Addiction

When we begin to focus our purpose and vision, it's necessary to incorporate balance, recognizing the difference between healthy sacrifice and debilitating obsession. "Many competent women have a difficult time distinguishing between passion and workaholism," cautions psychologist Anne Wilson Schaef. "Many of our role models for success are people who were willing to be devoured by their work. This is confusing to us. True passion and doing what is important for us to do does not require us to destroy ourselves in the process. In fact, it is when passion gets distorted to compulsivity that it is destructive."

She suggests this credo for compulsion-prone women: "My passion feeds me. My addictiveness devours me. There is a great difference between the two."[5] A passion fattens the soul; an addiction starves it. A passion brings a fuller, happier person to relationships; an addiction leads to discontentment and isolation. A passion serves God with an open, imaginative heart; an addiction shuts down vision and spirituality.

Addictive personalities respond well to the idea of passion; they understand the idea of "giving their all" to someone or something. But they lack the discernment and ability to draw appropriate boundaries around their commitments. They crave constant stimulation; balance and leisure don't belong to their vocabulary. If we use our life purpose to alter negative moods, prove our self-worth, or avoid what's painful, we've crossed the line from passion into addiction. We're seeking serenity from an object or event instead of God.

People who keep their life purpose in balance understand the priority of relationship. The book *The Addictive Personality* outlines four natural relationships we turn to for support, nurture, guidance, love, and emotional and spiritual growth. The author categorizes these relationships as family and friends, a spiritual Higher Power (whom we know to be God), the self, and community. If we don't develop healthy relationships in these areas, we turn to other sources to meet our needs.[6] This is how addiction begins, and if we're lacking in any of these areas, we should run, not walk, to those who can compassionately assist us with spiritually based recovery and relationship building.

If as wives and mothers we're pursuing a purpose in addition to our family, we need to gauge our passion against those of a husband and children. Their well-being takes priority over most pursuits, and I believe God honors decisions that place people above accomplishments. On the other hand, it also takes balance not to worship at the shrine of family to the exclusion of other relationships and responsibilities. It is possible to isolate ourselves within the family structure, hiding from personal growth and spiritual calling.

After years of reading biographies about women, I've observed that the most "successful" women have frequently been the most addictive. They've obsessively worked to the sacrifice of marriages, children, and friendships. Their greatest strengths have been matched by astounding weaknesses, and without a spiritual anchor in their lives, they don't heal themselves or their fractured relationships. I don't draw this comparison to discourage us from accomplishment, but to caution. As Christians, we can more wisely manage relationships if we continually listen to and obey the Holy Spirit's guidance within.

The Art of Risking

Whatever the Holy Spirit tells us, he eventually asks us to risk. He first asks us to live by faith instead of sight,[7] then he fashions a tailor-made risk based on our purpose and vision. What looks like risk to me may not appear as risk to others and vice versa, so we may feel alone in our initial, shaky steps toward focus. This is God arranging circumstances so we trust him, and only him, during a winnowing process.

For one woman, focus may mean setting up an accounting practice. For another, it could require devoting more time to advising younger women. To another, risk takes the shape of a moving van as she ventures a cross-country relocation. It could mean for two hours a day picking up the telephone and marketing our business or becoming the only full-time, stay-at-home mother in the neighborhood. What these risktakers share is God's insistence that we focus through his lens rather than our own and especially not through the optical illusions of our critics' opinions.

When we begin to focus, some people won't understand our decisions. "Everyone else is vying for management positions," they insist. (Or joining the coffee klatch, the film group, the Saturday night planning sessions.) Or the pleading voice in the church foyer believes this project has our name stamped on it. But if these involvements compete with our focus, we dilute the power of purpose by contaminating it with well-intentioned activities that keep us running in circles instead of straight toward our goal. We must learn to graciously say no.

When we say no, we spare ourselves and others from frustration, failure, or backtracking. Several years ago I agreed to participate on a conference committee, saying yes when I should have said no. I was already over my head in work, but the committee chairperson was persuasive, and the task of developing seminar topics appealed to my ego. Halfway through the committee's life I couldn't keep up and asked to resign. My request set off a fight between the chairperson and me and initiated a rocky transition of duties to a new seminar facilitator. I could have avoided it all by asking, "Does this involvement stick to my focus?"

We must learn to say no, but we can't stop there. We also must teach ourselves to say yes to what keeps us focused. This could be as basic as eating healthily, meditating on Scripture, or getting adequate sleep and exercise. It could be as transitional as revamping our schedule and workplace, attending skill-building classes, and giving the children more household chores. Or as daring as raising funds for a community project, serving on a committee with intimidating people, renting a hideaway cottage for a season, or jumping into an activity that stretches our abilities until they almost burst.

When focus commands us to say yes, to fling ourselves into unknown space, the internal and external protesters rise up again.

"You're going to do *what?*" "Don't ask for that. You'll never get it."
"Why can't you just take it easy? You deserve it." "Nobody else does
it that way." Consequently, we must say yes loudly enough so our souls
reverberate with the anticipation of a new adventure and drown out the
prattle. No waffling, no saying yes when we really mean no, no slack-
ing on our promises. No turning back.

Naomi didn't turn back when she searched inside and discovered
no passion left for her job as an art director. Although the coming years
promised attractive design challenges, they no longer fit her soul. Her
real desire was to become an art therapist, helping people articulate and
heal their emotional pain by expressing their feelings through art.

This new vision required risk and focus. No art therapy schools
existed within driving distance from her home, and Naomi's husband,
Curt, loved his job as a teacher. After researching the possibilities she
found a graduate school that required three summers of classes at an
out-of-state campus, interspersed with independent studies and
practicums in her local community. Curt agreed to the summertime
separations—a challenge to their close-knit marriage—and in her
early thirties Naomi retreated to a college dormitory, focusing on her
personally and intellectually terrifying goal.

Naomi's demeanor months after graduation proved the intense
focus and risk were worth it. I'd never seen her so at peace and full
of pleasure, so very much herself. In her last summer at the college,
Curt visited for a few days and Naomi got pregnant. Now she's on

another adventure, learning to balance the needs of a husband, daughter, and clients.

Naomi's story also demonstrates that focus must still remain fluid enough to accommodate daily tyrannies and unexpected life changes.

The Rhythm of Responsibilities

What we do on a daily basis adds up to a life that's either well used or wasted. Yet focusing on what matters the most each day doesn't imply just purchasing a time-management system and sticking to it. Rather, keeping focused involves responding to the rhythm of our responsibilities.

Perhaps I'm pushing my own preference, but to expect every woman to achieve focus in the same way denies her individuality, creativity, and chance for peak performance. If no two people are alike and each life purpose is unique, how can we expect everybody to manage their schedules in similar ways? We can learn from one another, we can implement methods and structures, but getting focused eventually narrows to designing the days to fit our personal style and situation.

A young woman whose purpose is "to raise God-loving children" spends her days immersed in caring for a family. This describes my niece Cathy's life. Focusing on purpose begins merely by opening her eyes in the morning to the sight of hungry, cherublike faces and subsides (but doesn't end) when four youngsters crawl into bed at night.

Dawn to dark, purpose surrounds her, creating a familiar and chaotic rhythm. The challenge isn't how to focus on her purpose, but how to get everything done—and how to snatch restful moments away from her focus.

At the other end of the spectrum are women like me. When *Clarity* was sold to a new publisher, I switched to working out of a home-based rather than a corporate office and working half-time instead of full-time on the magazine. I spend the rest of my time writing and serving editorial clients, and the variety combined with working at home has challenged my focus. I live alone, so nobody notices if I putter around the house instead of perch at my computer. I've finally admitted I'm highly distractible, and for me focus is a daily battle. For the love of my purpose, though, it is a war I want to win.

I'm gradually learning that my best writing times are in the morning or evening. Forget the afternoon; I might as well take a nap then, and sometimes I do. This fits my natural inclinations, and I've grown to realize that being available to my clients and getting the work done matter more than what other people think of my unorthodox schedule.

Between Cathy and me reside hosts of spiritual women who, to fulfill their purpose-filled vision, face the daily dilemma of focus. Many work nine-to-five jobs, and the bulk of a day's time is decided for them; other women working at home need to make hourly decisions about using their time. Yet we all can test our focus by asking, "Am I making steady progress in fulfilling my life purpose and current vision?" If we answer no, then the follow-up question becomes, "What needs to change?"

Freedom and Change

When we encounter the change process, we can emphasize what we'll lose to the exclusion of what we'll gain. If this outlook descibes us, we first need to adjust our attitude about change. When we make changes in favor of focus, we set ourselves free to reach God's best and highest purpose for us, meshed with the fulfillment of our desires. What could be more rewarding than that? Why would we resist change when it ushers in our dreams?

Perhaps it's because we're focused on worldly security, clutching what we can see instead of visualizing who we can be. But this is a false security, based on the temporal and unpredictable, and when it's compared to God's immutable and everlasting commitment to us, we bump against how security conscious we can be. We cling to jobs, homes, titles, habits, money, schedules, locations, relationships, involvements, and an abundance of *things* as if they were truly rewarding and eternal. Instead we must practice our "new way of seeing" through spiritual eyes to detect what has become an albatross, weighing us down and drowning purposeful progress.

To dissolve this resistance to change, the Bible advises us to "lay aside every weight, and the sin which doth so easily beset us, and...run with patience the race that is set before us. Looking unto Jesus the author and finisher of our faith; who for the joy that was set before him endured the cross, despising the shame, and is set down at the right hand of the throne of God."[8]

As Jesus did, we must set aside purpose-hindering weights to focus on the joy set before us, the joy of being all God created us to be, the wonder of doing all he's called us to do. This way of seeing casts a different light on change, the light of the Holy Spirit, and we can welcome rather than fear the adjustments that lead to focus.

These changes are individual, but universal in effect. Initially we can feel apprehensive about letting go; in retrospect we understand that loosening our grip is one of the best decisions we've ever made. Over the last decade at several junctures focus has required giving up what I cling to most: a secure job. When a position has no longer accommodated my growing purpose, God pushed me to move on. In two instances he terminated jobs to carry me, squirming and complaining, to the next level of focus. Each time the transition frightened me, but I look back and understand that every time God knew what he was doing. Sometimes when we're too afraid or inert to implement change, God starts the process for us.

In other cases change requires that we concentrate on it first before focusing on a purposeful vision. I have a friend who wants to pursue her purpose, but has set aside several months to rectify health problems that sap her energy. A different friend zeroed in on reducing personal debt. Other women walk toward focus by giving their marriages priority, assuring husbands that pursuing purpose doesn't mean neglecting them. The change that leads to focus looks, feels, and endures differently for everyone.

Accepting the Interruptions

Whatever we do to focus our lives, there's one everyday hindrance we can't change—the descent of interruptions. Hardly any woman's life can run as smoothly as she plans it in her daybook. Typically we are the relationship keepers, and people bring on errors, changes, illnesses, emergencies, emotional needs, and other surprises. There are also spiritual warfare, natural disasters, personal inconsistencies, and unexpected opportunities. It's tempting to grouse or worry about these departures and how they diffuse our focus, but this wastes emotional energy. We're more apt to keep our sanity and composure if we accept interruptions as the natural flow of life, padding time into our schedules for the unexpected. The reality of interruptions builds an even stronger case for focusing on one purpose and not spreading ourselves too thin.

Yet with planning and flexibility, some interruptions still throw us wildly off base. We can remind ourselves that God works all things together for good,9 and we can only do our best and leave the results to him. I've created a motto for when I fall into these situations: *Eventually everything gets done.* We meet the deadlines, the kids get clothes for the new school year, we wind up on that vacation after all. Life has a way of working itself out.

There are occasional times when tragedy or pressing needs elongate into a season of departure from our focus. Madalene dropped most everything when her husband slowly died from cancer. She focused solely on Harlan and doesn't regret pulling in and away from other people and responsibilities. Now three years later she and friends sense it's time to focus on her talent again, and I almost smell the anticipation. A mother who zeroes in on a flailing child wouldn't consider any other choice, and weathering a divorce or illness can numb us indefinitely. God understands and hovers during these departures, offering comfort and deepening our character and spirituality. He also taps a shoulder when it's time, despite the residual grief and pain, to rekindle our purposeful calling.

Another elongated interruption centers on our need for rest and spiritual refueling. Hopefully, we figure regular respites into the rhythm of our days, but there are times when taking care of ourselves during an extended period is all we can and should manage.

A Time for Everything

The general principle behind focus is overall balance. At times we must all-out focus on our purpose, stretching schedules and people as far as they'll bend without snapping. At times purpose retreats while we work through what's urgent. In between, we create a rhythm to our days that balances focus with rest, responsibility with relationship. Not taking on too much, not settling for too little.

King Solomon observed that in life there is a time for everything. As women of purpose, we can use his verse as a litany when we're sorting out focus.

There is a time for everything,

and a season for every activity under heaven:

a time to be born and a time to die,

a time to plant and a time to uproot,

a time to kill and a time to heal,

a time to tear down and a time to build,

a time to weep and a time to laugh,

a time to mourn and a time to dance,

a time to scatter stones and a time to gather them,

a time to embrace and a time to refrain,

a time to search and a time to give up,

a time to keep and a time to throw away,

a time to tear and a time to mend,

a time to be silent and a time to speak,

a time to love and a time to hate,

a time for war and a time for peace. [10]

Yes, there is a time for everything. And if we're willing to be shaped by the Master, there is even a time for brokenness.

Chapter Six

Brokenness

Facing Pain and Weakness

Jesus shares our suffering;
He nurses us and heals us by His own wounds and stripes.
As we go through our valleys, He keeps us constant company.
And that is what makes the difference.
His presence is our joy.

COLLEEN TOWNSEND EVANS

I PICKED UP THE GLASS on my office desk and hurled it at a wall several feet away. As shattered bits spread across the carpet, I choked, "This is insanity! Is this what I get for following you, God? *Is this it?*"

Slumping to the floor, I curled into a fetal position and sobbed. My dreams were smoldering, and I wanted to join the ashes. Just a few nights before I'd driven to the ocean with thoughts of wading in permanently. But imagining a grief-stricken family stopped me. So there I sat, in a dim office late at night, angry and afraid.

Eventually the tears gave way to a silent moan, and I pulled myself upright. And in my exhaustion and confusion, I felt more alarmed by a fresh dent in the wall than by my death wish. Dropping to the floor again, I shakily picked up bits of glass, hoping to destroy any evidence colleagues would question in the morning. As pieces plunked into the wastebasket, I thought, *This is how I feel, Lord. Broken. Do you shatter everyone who serves you?*

I had started with good intentions. Several years before I'd resigned a great secular job and, convinced of God's leading, left family and friends to enter religious publishing in another state. Soon after, life crumbled. I hated my job and apartment. It was tough finding friends outside of work. I'd accepted a salary cut, and money dwindled. My car disintegrated at the rate of a few hundred dollars each month. A potential romance fizzled. I developed health problems and sensed spiritual warfare. And I felt intensely lonely.

Numb and depressed from disappointment, I questioned: *Hadn't I felt God's definite leading? Hadn't I sacrificed to obey him? Wasn't this job related to my purpose? Then why was I so miserable?* The answers seemed embedded somewhere in each new difficulty, but I was too emotionally depleted to dig deep enough for them.

After a few years circumstances improved, although they never turned ideal, and I began to mentally formulate and ask God for my dream job. The hope of that ultimate goal had helped me persevere, and now that I'd "paid my dues," I felt certain God would answer my request and bless me. After all, I had obeyed and survived, even thrived. I was sticking to my purpose.

After much thought and prayer, I finally sensed a heavenly go-ahead on a position with another company. Although it meant another move, another set of adjustments, I was willing. *This* position was what I'd searched and struggled for; *this* would be God's good and perfect gift to me. And *this* was what dropped me to my knees, scuttling for broken bits of glass and fragments of myself.

Instead of entering the Promised Land, I fell into a lion's den, and eventually circumstances—and my ability to manage them—worsened. After eight months of employment my position terminated because of the company's financial status. I was stranded: no job in sight, no money or family to fall back on, no emotional reserve to cope, no trust that God would rescue me. Or at least not without torturing me.

Growing up I'd been taught that God has a perfect plan for my life, but when circumstances struck hard, that belief spun out of my hands, dented my wall of self-protection, and left me searching for meaning in the chaos. At first I considered the disappointments a cosmic joke. Now I call them a severe mercy, for with each jolt God has stretched, challenged, and grown me so I have a deeper understanding of the world, his ways, myself.

I still believe God directs our steps, but now I suspect he cares more about refining and strengthening character than orchestrating plans. So when we pursue our purpose, we're in for a ride that changes us more than anything or anybody else.

An Undying Myth

A persistent myth circulates among spiritually attuned people. It claims if we follow God's purpose and vision for us, we'll always wind up happily ever after. No pain or disappointment, no second-guessing ourselves and our circuitous destinations. Just smooth sailing toward the afterlife.

This myth persists because we want to believe it. We reason, "If God is good and perfect, can't he provide us with the good life? Doesn't he want to?" The answer on both counts is yes. He provided this perfect life in the Garden of Eden, but we foiled the plan. Because of our choice to sin, even redeemed humanity can't know perfection until we reach heaven, but the essence of an unencumbered existence haunts our spiritual memory. We sense that somewhere perfection was possible, and we live with the desire but not the capability to acquire seamless lives.

Despite our wishes, Jesus said in the world we will experience tribulation,[1] and this trouble arrives in many forms. Christians encounter divorce, illness, job loss, bankruptcy, death of loved ones, public humiliation, and every tribulation known to humanity. I could blithely say that "everything happens for a reason," but at times a justifiable reason is as impossible to grasp as the smoke of our cindered lives.

I pondered this lately after hearing about the trials of two friends. After surviving a messy divorce and a mystifying long-term illness, Laurie found her heart's delight in Joey, a charming man who proposed marriage. Anticipating their nuptials, Laurie moved to his city in another state and began planning the wedding, but within a few months Joey had second thoughts and called everything off. Laurie, who had uprooted from a job, family, and friends, is now devastated and stranded, without a familiar shoulder to cry on.

More incomprehensible is what has happened to Mary. In her twenties she married Craig, only to be abandoned by him within a year. In her thirties she dated another man for several years but stalled on accepting his marriage proposal. Just when Mary decided to say yes, he died in a job-related accident. Later, in her forties, she dated another man a decade older than she. After a few years he proposed marriage, and before Mary finally agreed, this boyfriend suddenly died from a heart attack.

Both of these cherishable women love God and desire his purpose for their lives, and in my estimation neither of them deserves tragedy. If I were Laurie, I'd feel divinely forsaken; if Mary, I'd feel cursed. As I pray for them, I plead that they not lose their faith, that they understand how sin debilitates our once-perfect world and the people in it, that they realize these tragedies didn't happen because they're "bad" or unworthy of good things. I ask God to show himself in spectacular ways to these women so they know he has not betrayed them.

Their grief reminds me of my years of disappointment—different in circumstance but still pain provoking. I often thought, *God doesn't love me as he loves other people. He has good things for everyone else but me.* Looking back, I adamantly label this untrue. I can trace his protective and generous hand throughout those years, but at the time, tears and mistrust clouded my eyes.

In retrospect I understand that God grieves with us and cares deeply about our brokenheartedness. Often he does not eradicate a difficulty but abides with us through it, whether or not we sense his presence. He longs to comfort and heal us, turning our ashes into beauty, our mourning into joy, our weakness into praise.[2] He wants to use the pain to make us more holy, pliable, credible, and compassionate as we fulfill our purpose.

Finding One's Own Soul

In the novel *The Chosen* Danny grows up as a child of Reb Saunders, the religious leader of a Hasidic sect of Jews in Williamsburg. Being the eldest son, Danny is expected to follow in his father's footsteps as the community's *tzaddick.* Since Danny's childhood his father has not spoken directly to him but has only communicated with him through other people.

When Danny graduates from high school, Reb Saunders finally breaks the silence after explaining to his son's friend Reuven why he's stayed remote from the child he loves dearly. At four years old Danny's brilliant mind devoured a book and recited it back from memory. "I went away and cried to the Master of the Universe," recalls Reb Saunders. "What have you done to me? A mind like this I need for a son? A *heart* I need for a son, a *soul* I need for a son, *compassion* I need from my son, righteousness, mercy, strength to suffer and carry pain, that I want from my son, not a mind without a soul!"

Without such a soul, Reb Saunders feared his son would be a haughty leader of the people, a *tzaddick* who couldn't empathize and intercede for their suffering. He didn't want a son without a soul; a son without a soul would be a shell of a man.

To Reuven he explained his theology of good and evil. "A man is born into this world with only a tiny spark of goodness in him. The spark is God, it is the soul; the rest is ugliness and evil, a shell. The spark must be guarded like a treasure, it must be nurtured, it must be fanned into flame. It must learn to seek out other sparks, it must dominate the shell. Anything can be a shell, Reuven. Anything. Indifference, laziness, brutality, and genius. Yes, even a great mind can be a shell and choke the spark."

So Reb Saunders taught his son with silence though it pained both of them. "One learns of the pain of others by suffering one's own pain, by turning inside oneself, by finding one's own soul," Reb Saunders' father had told him. "And it is important to know of pain. It destroys our self-pride, our arrogance, our indifference toward others. It makes us aware of how frail and tiny we are and of how much we must depend upon the Master of the Universe."[3]

When life's events and relationships turn sour, it can feel as though God practices a similar silence with us. Yet he has not forgotten us. Even if we can't hear him, the Father walks alongside and consoles us, but still allows the circumstances to deepen our character. I imagine God feeling the pain, just as Danny's father did with him.

"In the silence between us, [Danny] began to hear the world crying," declared Reb Saunders with a long, trembling sigh like a moan.[4] Because of his own pain, Danny would serve not only with his talent, but also from a depthful soul.

This is God's desire for us, too.

Traveling the Wasteland

To the unholy mind suffering squanders talent, but to be spiritually useful to God we must periodically travel the wasteland of brokenness. In this desert God tenderly picks up our shattered pieces and remolds them into the image of his Son. During the redesign he promises, "A bruised reed [I] will not break, and a smoldering wick [I] will not snuff out."[5] No matter how broken we feel, God won't allow the pain to destroy us.

During one season of suffering, while driving to church I complained to God that he was wasting my talents. "This job is too small for me and not what I had in mind for my purpose," I told him. "Why do you insist on keeping me here? I hate it." Almost instantly these words flashed through my mind: *Poured out as a drink offering.*

Later at home, in the Scriptures I pinpointed this statement from the apostle Paul to the Philippians: "But even if I am being poured out like a drink offering on the sacrifice and service coming from your faith, I am glad and rejoice with all of you."[6] In the Old Testament God's people presented drink offerings of oil and wine along with various sacrifices for purifying themselves from sin or entering into fellowship with God.[7] To pour out an expensive wine before the Lord was a holy task; what appeared to man as a waste of a fine product was an act of consecration to God.

While Paul mentored Timothy, the elder missionary admonished the young man to fulfill his ministry. Then the apostle proclaimed, "For I am already being poured out like a drink offering, and the time has come for my departure. I have fought the good fight, I have finished the race, I have kept the faith."[8] Paul apparently considered his role as a drink offering a lifetime commitment, played out at difficult points in his ministry. From his example we can remind ourselves that a purposeful life fills with both pleasure and pain.

The periodic pain of "fighting the good fight" prepares us for serving others, for we, too, are to be poured out for the Lord's service like costly drink offerings. This "pouring out" is the *sine qua non,* the essential ingredient, of spiritual vision and the reason God wants us to search for purpose and passion in the first place. We are to use our valuable talents in the humble service of others, wiping their feet with the sweet aroma of our abilities.

"So must we, modern women that we are, learn to become hand-maidens of the Lord," explains author Karen Burton Mains. "It is not until we offer ourselves up completely, not until we give up our rights, not until we seek first the will of this Divine Lord, that we can know the meaning of giving birth to holy things—whether the children of our hearts or minds or hands."9 As we suffer, we give up our rights for God's will and we serve with reverence instead of selfish ambition.

When it dawned on me that God was spilling out my life as a drink offering, I sniffed and replied, "You've got to be kidding! Haven't I given up enough already?" I didn't want my purpose wasted on humble tasks. I felt destined for greater things, and sometimes I wonder if my prideful attitude added a few more years to my pain and preparation. God commits to completing his character work within us, and if we don't "get it" the first time, he might oblige us with the same painstaking lesson again and again until he wears off our rough edges. A spiritual mentor of mine calls this "trudging around the mountain again." Looking back, I've taken enough round trips to make a mountaineer dizzy.

Loosening Besetting Sins

Suffering doesn't just result from circumstances beyond our control; we also feel pain from our sins, and perhaps this is the deepest grief of all. For me it's easier to manage external difficulties than my internal failings and personal transgressions. When I sin, I can't pass the guilt to anyone else.

Sin compromises our relationship with God and the full pursuit of purpose. I'm not referring to the assorted daily sins we confess and throw away, although it's important to cleanse ourselves from these. I refer to the besetting sins, the repeated transgressions we can't release, the addictions that trouble and isolate us. God wants to use this pain to change us, too.

A friend who's a therapist says when clients feel pain, it's the opportune time for them to confront their wrongdoing. Pain makes us vulnerable, open to assistance, and sick of our wickedness. It's a ripe time to "let go and let God" extricate the sin that entangles us and plant our feet on the narrow path.

Once when I cried to God about chronic emotional pain, in my mind's eye I saw a heart wrapped in a network of thorny vines. *This is your heart,* whispered God. *It's dying from the sin that's choking it.* He didn't have to name the sin; I knew the disobedience that strangled my spirit. I'd love to say I immediately gave this besetting sin to God, but it took years for me to let go, bit by bit. Like people who've fought addiction, I still consider myself as "recovering." I know at any time Satan can tempt me with this sin's allure and without God's help I could regress. So I remind myself how this would grieve God and con-taminate the effectiveness of my purpose. For the love of both, I need to keep walking away from sin.

While besetting sins compromise our purpose by rendering us less effective or blocking it altogether, at the same time God is patient and long-suffering.[10] If he waited for our perfection, the Creator wouldn't have anyone to do his work in the world. I think the key is whether we're "walking away" or "walking toward" sin. If we're willing to confess and repent (turn away) from sin, God patiently works in us amid our purpose-filled activities. "Because of the LORD's great love we are not consumed, for his compassions never fail. They are new every morning."[11] If we stubbornly disobey, he might set us aside for an overhaul. Think of Jonah.[12]

Still, I offer this distinction between "walking away" and "walking toward" as a guideline, not an absolute. Who can know the mind of God? He works uniquely with each person, and often he's more merciful than humans. When I've felt battered and broken from sin, God has been his most tender. The kindness of God can lead us to repentance,[13] yet I don't advocate testing "how far we can go" before he disciplines us. We are not to tempt the Lord our God. Remember what happened to Ananias and Sapphira.[14]

Purpose aside, the primary reason for abandoning sin is our access to a holy God. He is the lover of our souls, and sin hampers communication with him. The psalmist straightforwardly explained, "I cried out to him with my mouth; his praise was on my tongue. If I had cherished sin in my heart, the Lord would not have listened."[15] If we never found or fulfilled our purpose, we'd still battle sin to keep our conscience clear, to enjoy an unfettered relationship with him. This clarity of conscience also helps us serve with boldness, unafraid of what critics might dig up and throw our way.

"Who is going to harm you if you are eager to do good? But even if you should suffer for what is right, you are blessed," Peter told the Christians of Asia Minor. "But in your hearts set apart Christ as Lord...keeping a clear conscience, so that those who speak maliciously against your good behavior in Christ may be ashamed of their slander. It is better, if it is God's will, to suffer for doing good than for doing evil."[16]

In Praise of Weakness

During twenty-plus years in the work force I've enrolled in seminars and conferences designed to improve my job performance. I've learned time-saving tips, budgeting shortcuts, communication skills, management strategies, and minutiae I've forgotten when I hit the parking lot. After devoting hundreds of hours and dollars to instruction, I'd say the underlying theme of these sessions has been "Don't let them see you sweat." In the marketplace—in our world—we're consumed with concealing our weaknesses.

As a young employee I swallowed this advice whole, but these days I'm mulling over how it contradicts Scripture. In the Sermon on the Mount, Christ described the traits of his followers. They're qualities our culture for the most part doesn't respect because we associate them with weakness. Consider these contrasts between Christ's beatitudes in Matthew 5:3—10 and the world's values.

Beatitude	Worldly Value	God's Reward
Poor in spirit	Pride and independence	Kingdom of heaven
Mourning	Happiness at any cost	Comfort
Meekness	Power	Inherit the earth
Righteousness	Personal needs	Filled (satisfied)
Mercy	Strength without feeling	Be shown mercy
Pure in heart	Deception	See God
Peacemaker	Personal peace without regard for others	Be called children of God
Persecuted	Weak commitments	Inherit the kingdom of heaven [17]

Christ loves and honors the lowly, the downtrodden, the weak. And this is good news for people like me. Though I've tried to look strong and capable, I've often felt insufficient and panicky. From learning to swim in junior high to teaching my first journalism class to launching a magazine, I've exclaimed, "I can't do this! I'm not strong enough." And with each admission I've tapped into a brokenness set apart from tragedy or sinfulness—the brokenness of inadequacy.

When we pursue purpose, we'll eventually bump against overwhelming situations that expose how weak we really are. We feel bereft and inadequate, and contrary to our culture's demands, this is precisely how God wants us to feel so we'll depend on him. When we finally grasp this concept, it's a relief to drop our facade of rugged individualism, admit that we're weak, and allow him to guide and strengthen us.

Paul pushed this concept further by suggesting we delight in our weakness. When he petitioned God to remove his "thorn in the flesh," the Lord replied, "My grace is sufficient for you, for my power is made perfect in weakness." So Paul decided, "I will boast all the more gladly about my weaknesses, so that Christ's power may rest on me. That is why, for Christ's sake, I delight in weaknesses, in insults, in hardships, in persecutions, in difficulties. For when I am weak, then I am strong."[18]

God specializes in taking the "weaklings" of the world and turning them into strong and beautiful souls. In his eyes brokenness is not a failure; it is the gateway to deeper spirituality.

In the allegory *Hinds' Feet on High Places,* the Shepherd asks Much-Afraid to join him on a climb to the High Places. At the journey's end she recalls how he lovingly treated her as she struggled to overcome weaknesses. "You, my Lord, never regarded me as I actually was, lame and weak and crooked and cowardly," she began. "You saw me as I would be when you had done what you promised and had brought me to the High Places, when it could be truly said, 'There is none that walks with such a queenly ease, nor with such grace, as she.' You always treated me with the same love and graciousness as though

I were a queen already."[19] When we confess our inadequacy, we give God the opportunity to express his graciousness to and through us.

A Peaceable Harvest

One reason God is gracious toward our difficulties, sin, and weakness is because Jesus Christ, his only son, suffered similar pain and temptations while on the earth. Christ's purpose was to seek and save the lost, and to accomplish this mission he accepted a horrible death by crucifixion. On the cross he bore the punishment for our sins so we can accept his gift of blood-stained salvation and exchange eternal damnation for everlasting life.

Each time I read of Christ's final affliction, I'm moved by how much grief he bore—certainly more agony than I'll face in a lifetime. The prophet Isaiah poetically predicted Christ's suffering:

He was despised and rejected by men,

a man of sorrows, and familiar with suffering.

Like one from whom men hide their faces

he was despised, and we esteemed him not.

Surely he took up our infirmities

and carried our sorrows,

yet we considered him stricken by God,

smitten by him, and afflicted.

But he was pierced for our transgressions,

he was crushed for our iniquities;

the punishment that brought us peace *was upon him,*
     and by his wounds we are healed. [20]

Christ agonized on the cross to redeem us, but also to bring a purity of heart and a peace that passes all understanding. God is good and wants to instill his goodness in us.

Crying in my office that terrible night, I couldn't imagine anything good emerging from my pain. I didn't understand that purpose is about being as much as doing, and the surest route to character development is the tunnel of difficulty.

Scripture reminds us that "no discipline seems pleasant at the time, but painful. Later on, however, it produces a harvest of *righteousness and peace* for those who have been trained by it." [21]

And for this harvest, he teaches us to persevere.

Chapter Seven

Perseverance

Plodding Ahead with Heart and Hope

&

What then should we be?
That each will answer for himself.
But for myself and to myself I say:
Though stripped of every armor, be a warrior—
a warrior of the spirit, for what the spirit knows.

DOROTHY THOMPSON

WHEN GUESTS ENTER the grounds next to the Casa del Alfarero ministry, they're warned to brace themselves for the filth and stench so nobody vomits. Throwing up a meal insults the people living there, although it's precisely what visitors would like to do. Fortunately the senses eventually acclimate, and most guests don't offend the land-fill's residents.

Yes, the landfill. The city dump.

Amid rotted chicken and soiled diapers, the poorest of the poor who live in this, one of Guatemala City's garbage dumps, scavenge for scraps to eat. Picking through the trash, both young and old search for plastic containers and ripped cardboard to recycle for small change. Just above them hundreds of purplish black vultures circle the sky, perusing for carcasses and diving at leftovers.

Into this decaying world stride Gladys and Lisbeth, two Guatemalan women who traded their comfortable counseling careers for a spiritual outreach to the "dump people."

"A lot of my friends thought I was crazy," remembers Gladys. "For several years we didn't have any volunteers. I tried recruiting young people from my church, but a brother in the church told them not to help because of the danger. Others thought we'd catch a disease. People thought it was a phase and we'd get over it."

But Gladys and Lisbeth didn't get over it. Instead they forged ahead, and the ministry burgeoned. Now they work with more than thirty volunteers, mostly teenagers, and accept food and financial contributions from local churches and an international Christian relief organization. The Casa's pharmacy gets stocked with the best medical supplies in the city, and with their staff the women manage a medical and dental clinic, offer carpentry and sewing classes, teach Bible lessons, and serve hunger-defying meals. It's often depressing and discouraging, but it's what Gladys and Lisbeth feel compelled to do and where they want to be.

"For me it's real what the Word of God says that he who gives to the poor gives to God," explains Gladys. "There are a lot of promises from God for those who give to the poor. That's why I tell people we have nothing, but we have everything."

Both Gladys and Lisbeth receive invitations to teach or work with other ministries, but their hearts stay buried in the dump. These women can't envision their lives away from Casa del Alfarero's needy residents, and they dream about the people's future.

"I ask the Lord to not let me die until I see spiritual revival here," says Lisbeth. "We've been planting seeds for several years and I would like to see the [people] seek the Lord sincerely. That is my desire, to see a spiritual revival here, because I know that's the exit to their pain and suffering."

Gladys agrees and embellishes the dream. "A lot of the kids think this is where they belong, but I would like to see some of them become professionals and marry good people. I'd like to see one of our girls in a white dress getting married in a church. I'd like to see our kids discipling others. I'd like to see..."[1]

Starting Out Right

Gladys and Lisbeth unmistakably know their purpose in life, and this heart-based knowledge affords them fulfillment and a sense of destiny, even when their efforts haven't yet produced rewards.

Gladys and Lisbeth know how to persevere.

Not many people do these days. We've become a society of disposable commitments. Like trash in a dump, we discard marriages and education, children and memberships, jobs and friends, churches and projects because we don't feel like trying anymore. We abandon our goals and dreams before they come true and wonder why our lives aren't satisfying, why so few things last.

Part of the problem is we don't start out right. If a couple adopts a "let's see how this works out" attitude toward their marriage, the union is probably doomed from the beginning. The same is true for other involvements, including the pursuit of purpose. When God places a purpose and vision within us, we'll accomplish nothing of spiritual significance by dabbling. We need to commit. In the Old Testament Moses instructed the Israelites, "Whatever your lips utter you must be sure to do, because you made your vow freely to the LORD your God with your own mouth."[2] This is wise advice for us, too—not to discourage us from proclaiming our purpose but to choose carefully.

An act of consecration can declare before God that we're serious about our purpose. To consecrate our purpose we could write a mission statement in a journal or hold a private dedication service with a friend. We might inscribe a motivational scripture on a plaque or write a letter of commitment and read it aloud to God. A family could celebrate with a special meal or activity; a study group could devote time to commissioning prayer.

Recently I heard about a couple who dedicated their new home as a place to fulfill their God-designed purposes. They invited a church elder, family, and friends to a time of prayer, music, and blessings, and in their presence the couple consecrated the house for ministering to others and honoring the Lord before all who visit there.

When a volunteer group accepted two new workers, veteran

members consecrated the newcomers at a welcoming party. For both volunteers involvement in the project flowed from a life purpose, and somebody recognized this. As the two women sat, encircled by the others, senior members commissioned the women from Psalm 20.

Verses four and five were particularly meaningful:

May he [God] give you the desire of your heart
and make all your plans succeed.
We will shout for joy when you are victorious
and will lift up our banners in the name of our God.
May the LORD grant all your requests.

Whatever we do, an act of consecration works best when it combines writing out a purpose and verbalizing it to at least one person. These actions move our purpose from an idea into reality. Yet we shouldn't let the idea of commitment paralyze us, fearing we'll choose the wrong direction. Such fear overlooks the understanding, forgiving, revitalizing nature of God. He discerns between sincere misguidance and indifferent disobedience.

Paul Tournier, a medical doctor who wrote classics about faith and meaning, explained, "To seek the meaning of things and God's will does not spare us either from error or from doubt," he wrote, "nor does it resolve all the mysteries of our destiny, all the insoluble problems [caused] by any event in nature or in our lives; nevertheless, it does give a new meaning to our lives."[3]

This meaning inspires us to persevere.

Wrapping in Delight

I've met many remarkable women, but the friend who's influenced me the most has modeled unwavering commitment and perseverance. I've known Nancy more than twenty years, and during that time she's firmly pursued her destiny as a pianist, although she's talented in several areas. Into adulthood she's sacrificed time, money, involvements, and child-bearing for the joy of music, practicing hour upon hour to sensitively interpret a composer's work. She imparts this devotion to her piano students, and when she performs a concert, the single-mindedness pays off. Each time I hear Nancy play, I am awestruck.

Nancy doesn't persevere at the piano out of duty or workaholism. She plays for the sheer love of it. If she quit the lessons with her master teacher, if a student never entered her studio, if the concert schedule dried up, she'd still play. Nancy's wrapped in the delight of her purpose, and pursuing any other mission would be unthinkable.

Contrary to Nancy's life, some people think of perseverance as a negative experience, thrust upon them by unpleasant circumstances and the lack of choice. As a society we're not anchored to a value system that respects endurance or the pleasure of delayed and long-term rewards. Instant gratification propels us to settle for what's quick and easy, yet this approach doesn't reflect God's character. The Bible says God's name, love, word, mercy, faithfulness, and righteousness endure forever.[4] He commits to us eternally because he loves us unconditionally, and if his Spirit resides within, shouldn't we reflect his enduring character? Like a mother with her child, wouldn't we persevere for love's sake?

True and resilient perseverance springs from within, propelling us forward through peaks and valleys, joy and despair. When our purpose explodes with fulfillment, perseverance shouts, "Isn't this grand?" When we're faced with discouragement, it whispers, "Keep going. This is what you're meant to do."

I wouldn't claim this unless I'd experienced those whispers myself. During the pressured years of developing and launching a magazine, I weathered so many setbacks that well-meaning friends suggested, "Why don't you quit? Everyone will understand if you do." On several occasions I wanted to resign and had good reason for it. Yet when the rumbles of each quake subsided, I heard a still, small voice within, saying, "Don't give up. Don't give up. Look what you'll miss if you do." And after I rested and reflected, my joy and passion returned.

Keeping the Faith

In regard to our spiritual walk Scripture speaks of enduring until the end, but the reasons we "keep the faith" also justify why we persevere through the delays and difficulties, sacrifices and celebrations of a life purpose.

Why do we persevere? Think about the following biblical reasons.

Reason	Scripture
Continuing unfinished work	These were all commended for their faith, yet none of them received what had been promised. God had planned something better for us so that only together with us would they be made perfect. Therefore, since we are surrounded by such a great cloud of witnesses,...let us run with perseverance the race marked out for us.—Hebrews 11:39–12:1
Earthly blessings	We consider blessed those who have persevered. You have heard of Job's perseverance and have seen what the Lord finally brought about. The Lord is full of compassion and mercy.—James 5:11
Discipline	Endure hardship as discipline; God is treating you as sons. For what son is not disciplined by his father? —Hebrews 12:7
Eternal reward	Blessed is the man that endureth temptation: for when he is tried, he

shall receive the crown of life.
—James 1:12a, KJV

Influence

Don't let anyone look down on you
because you are young, but set an
example for the believers in speech,
in life, in love, in faith and in purity....
Be diligent in these matters; give your-
self wholly to them, so that everyone
may see your progress.... Persevere in
them.—1 Timothy 4:12, 15—16

Joy

Let us fix our eyes on Jesus, the
author and perfecter of our faith, who
for the joy set before him endured
the cross.—Hebrews 12:2a

Personal redemption

But he who stands firm to the end
will be saved.—Matthew 24:13

Pleasing God

And we pray...that you may live a life
worthy of the Lord and may please
him in every way: bearing fruit in every
good work, growing in the knowledge
of God, being strengthened with all
power...so that you may have great

endurance and patience.
—Colossians 1:10—11

Salvation for others

Therefore I endure everything for the sake of the elect, that they too may obtain the salvation that is in Christ Jesus, with eternal glory.—2 Timothy 2:10

Spiritual maturity

Consider it pure joy, my brothers, whenever you face trials of many kinds, because you know that the testing of your faith develops perseverance. Perseverance must finish its work so that you may be mature and complete, not lacking anything.—James 1:2—4

Spiritual service

Endure hardship with us like a good soldier of Christ Jesus.—2 Timothy 2:3

Before embarking on our purpose, it helps to list and study our reasons for persevering so when hardship hits we can remind ourselves why we're not giving up. The one reason that underscores all of our justifications, however, is that God asks us to obey him. He considers obedience better than sacrifice[5] and wants us to pursue his purpose for us, his way instead of ours.

"God continually challenges us to act on our commitment.... What will we do with God's instruction? How will we build into our lives the active demonstration of commitment through obedience? How will we handle what God has shown us?" asks Martha Thatcher, a spiritual mentor to women.[6]

Hopefully, we'll obey through perseverance.

Piling Up Stones

Sometimes when God asks us to persevere, saying yes feels like traveling blindfolded. Before we step forward, we can look back at his past trustworthiness for encouragement and motivation. Then while traveling, we can build memorials to new expressions of his constancy.

Memorial building isn't a new idea. God knows we need assurances of his presence and assistance, so he created symbolic reminders for us like the rainbow and the cross. And at specific points in history he has asked people to build memorials according to his instructions.

When Joshua led the Israelites across the Jordan River into the promised land, God wanted his people to remember they'd crossed on dry ground. As they walked between parted waters, one man from each tribe hoisted a stone from the riverbed and carried it to the Canaan bank. They fashioned the twelve stones into a memorial and piled another dozen in the riverbed where priests had shouldered the ark of the covenant.

"Let this be a sign among you...," declared Joshua. "Because the waters of the Jordan were cut off before the ark of the covenant of the LORD...so these stones shall become a memorial to the sons of Israel forever."[7] The stones symbolized God's faithfulness.

For us a memorial can be as unique as our situation, as creative as our imagination. It can be as brief as a few words noted in a Bible, as sustained as a litany of praise. It can be private or public, planned or spontaneous, simple or elaborate. But always our memorial represents how God has helped us.

For years I've tucked a small "memorial" notebook in my bedroom nightstand. It contains Scripture promises, prophetic and encouraging words from people, and notations about God's faithfulness in fulfilling my purpose. When I'm downhearted or afraid of the next step, I review the notebook for encouragement. I know of one work group that keeps a scrapbook of photos and mementos to remind employees of past accomplishments, and another that records a "Scripture history" of God's guidance during critical passages in their ministry. Each time the group faces a major decision, looking at promises from the Bible—and their fulfillment—prepares them for the future.

Or memorial building can be as basic as noting a tree's growth in the backyard:

"Look how much the tree has grown."

"Yes, and think what it represents to us. How much we've been through…"

We especially need this affirmation in the thick of spiritual warfare, when we're working hard but reaping few or no results, or when God allows the death of a vision.

Roaring like a Lion

When I left my secular job for Christian publishing and fell headlong into disappointment, for months I fought confusion, depression, and a loss of identity and motivation. My prayers reduced to "God, help me" and "Please deliver me!" I chanted them like a rosary, hoping he would open up employment for me back in my hometown. I was convinced this new job caused my misery.

God did deliver me, but not in the way I expected. One Sunday a woman from my church invited me to lunch at her place, and as I consented, I sensed it would be an unusual afternoon. About this, I was right. After our meal Sandy prayed and told the evil spirits pestering me to leave. She never raised her voice or created a fanfare. She just gently held me and in the name of Jesus told them to flee.

When Sandy finished praying, peace had replaced the confusion, contentment had banished the pain. As we sat together in a church service that evening, I thought of the Gerasene demoniac who was "in his right mind" after Jesus delivered him from evil spirits.[8] Though I hadn't been possessed, I knew what it felt like to be "out of my mind" with hopelessness. I've never felt that confused again.

That night I concluded I'd been under spiritual attack. I'd taken steps to obey God's call to ministry, and Satan fought to drive me back. I had failed to recognize his tactics, believing my despair resulted from a failure to "buck up" in a new and tough situation. Then when I sensed his presence, I forgot that the devil prowls like a roaring lion9 but can't hurt me if I'm spiritually armed. I'd heard his roar, seen the paws waiting to pounce, and stood frozen in my tracks.

"The roaring of the king of beasts is an awesome and fear-producing sound, particularly if you happen to be the target for devouring," explains Mark Bubeck, a pastor specializing in spiritual warfare. "An old lion will often get on one side of the prey and roar vociferously, producing fear in the prey and causing it to run toward the younger lions waiting in ambush to leap out and kill the victim.... The roar of a lion can actually paralyze some prey when he stalks, causing the victim to be an early target for destruction. The same is true of believers who are the target for Satan's devouring. If he can create fear in us, we are much easier prey for him to destroy. Christians greatly err when they avoid the subject of spiritual warfare because of the fearsome power of Satan."10

We must understand that the old lion has a frightening roar but limited power to destroy us or our purpose. When we put on the "full armor of God" designed for spiritual warfare, we protect ourselves from that power, and he runs away. Our spiritual armor consists of the belt of truth, a breastplate of righteousness, shoes molded from the gospel of peace, a shield of faith, and the helmet of salvation.11 Spiritually speaking, it's socially acceptable to wear this same outfit every day; in fact, it's a must if we're to keep Satan and his forces at bay, unable to sink his teeth and claws into our purpose.

And we must pray—for protection, endurance, and the hope of a harvest when the first seeds haven't sprouted yet.

Sowing without Reaping

As a gardener I've picked the wrong place to live. Colorado (or at least my yard) has sandy soil, unpredictable weather, and a short growing season, so planting seeds becomes a game of roulette. A flower lover never knows what or how much she's going to get.

For the most part I reduce the odds by purchasing plants at the local nursery, but my neighbor—patient woman that she is—plunks seeds in the earth and waits until August to see results. But her garden isn't always showy. One year her front-yard flower bed flourishes with assorted colors and shapes; the next year it's spotty at best. I admire her persistence though. She's a pragmatist reconciled to the possibility of sowing without reaping.

In contrast each year I spend hundreds of dollars to smell flowers in June. Yet even this investment doesn't guarantee a breathtaking garden with the uncertainty of unseasonable weather, insects and mildew, neighborhood animals and neglect if I'm busy with other projects. So why bother?

Every spring I fill with hope that I'll grow a voluptuous garden and friends will marvel at nature's spectacular handiwork in my backyard. Thanks to this hope, as far-fetched as it may seem, I keep gardening. And this perseverance has taught me to love horticulture's process as much as its rewards.

Likewise, God wants us to harbor a wild hope when we sow the seeds of our purpose. Through years of preparation, through times of inconsistent or nonexistent results, he asks that we persevere for the joy of our purpose and love for him. God desires that, like natural-born gardeners, we find satisfaction in the process of our purpose—obeying, serving, growing—and leave the outcome to him. He may even test our perseverance when we have no results at all.

Gladys and Lisbeth from Casa del Alfarero know what "no results" feels like. "There are times I tell God, forget it, I can't keep going," admits Gladys. "You're left asking, 'God, can you really change these [people]?'"

But speaking for both of them, Lisbeth adds, "When we don't see changes, we still must maintain obedience to God. The Lord calls us to plant and bless independently of the results."

Hebrews 11 relates many biblical people who persevered and lived by faith but didn't receive the reward they'd hoped for. The writer of Hebrews explains: "All these people were still living by faith when they died. They did not receive the things promised; they only saw them and welcomed them from a distance. And they admitted that they were aliens and strangers on earth. People who say such things show that they are looking for a country of their own. If they had been thinking of the country they had left, they would have had opportunity to return. Instead, they were longing for a better country—a heavenly one. Therefore God is not ashamed to be called their God, for he has prepared a city for them."[12]

The pursuit of purpose reaches another level of maturity when we keep our hands to the plow but our eyes on heaven.

Trusting Life's Cycles

When we mature in our faith and purpose, like the master gardener we learn to trust and cooperate with the natural course of life. Throughout nature there's a cyclical pattern of dying to eventually spring back with newness. In the fall I cut down, cover up, and abandon the flower beds. In December it looks as though they'll never bloom again. Yet in July they burst with beauty if I exercise faith and perseverance during the months between.

Jesus said that unless a grain of wheat falls to the ground and dies, it will never yield a harvest. So it is with our purpose. Often before fulfilling a vision, God cuts down the dream and buries it in a faith-building process that feels like death. Reminiscent of Abraham raising a knife to slay his beloved son, God may test our true motivation by wresting away what we cherish the most.[13] Then he expects us to love and obey him faithfully during a dark season frequently called the death of a vision. When he's proved the vision is his and not ours to control, often he resurrects the dream and hands it to us, more beautiful and bountiful than we'd imagined—a product of the dormant and difficult days of a winter past.

The faith-invoking part of this ordeal is that we don't know if God will resurrect the dream. Sometimes he renews a vision. Sometimes he replaces it with another vision. Sometimes he asks us to let it go.

In her book *Jesus, CEO*, Laurie Beth Jones offers this memorable insight into letting go.

In one of the movies about Indiana Jones, he and his father are pursuing the Holy Grail. After many adventures and heartaches, Indiana is finally at the precipice—about to grasp the very item he and his father have been searching for. And yet, so precarious is his position on the cliff that his father realizes if Indiana retrieves the grail, he will lose his balance and fall into the pit below. As Indiana is about to lift up the prize, his father whispers, "Let it go." There is a long pause, and you can see the anguish in Indiana's face. Have they come all this way for nothing? Can't he finally grasp the treasure they've been searching for? Can't he finally make his father proud of him? Another second passes, and his father takes his arm and says more firmly, "Indiana, let it go."

Indiana does as he is instructed and the audience gasps. It is so un-Indiana like—so un-American, so un-Hollywood—that they should come all this way for nothing. And yet almost instantly the audience begins to realize that the trip wasn't about getting the grail. It was about spending time together on the journey—about being all tied up and facing death together and emerging with a stronger relationship. That was the prize.[14]

As spiritually attuned women who pursue purpose, our prize extends beyond strong human relationships, though these are great rewards in themselves. Perseverance yields an inner satisfaction that lasts, but, even more, the thrill of hearing our Creator say, "Well done."

Perseverance also ushers us into a position of influence, and this is purpose's long-awaited goal.

Chapter Eight

Influence

Reaching Out to Make a Difference

≶

Everyone reaches, but not everyone touches....
Reaching is instinctive;
but for the most part touching is learned.
For in touching we give and receive, talk and listen,
share ourselves and see into another.
And not everyone can do that or will do it.

GAIL MACDONALD

IN ONE OF MY FIRST "official" positions of influence I stumbled into
a conflict I'll never forget. Around age sixteen I wrote and directed a
play produced by my church's youth group, and on the Saturday
before a Sunday evening performance for our small congregation, the
thespians among us met at church for an overdue rehearsal.

Despite our eleventh-hour gathering the rehearsal progressed
smoothly, until I decided the play would fare better if we performed
in the basement instead of the sanctuary. (I've forgotten the reason I
considered this a clever idea.) Not many agreed, but I thought being

their leader meant doing things my way, so cast members begrudgingly hauled the homespun props downstairs, including a couch that barely passed through a narrow stairwell.

Within minutes of carting everything downstairs I figured the basement wasn't the right place after all. (I've always needed to see furniture arranged before I settle on it.) *Okay, let's move things back upstairs,* I decided. It made sense to me, but articulating my decision instigated a fallout. The guys especially felt annoyed because they'd carried the heavy pieces.

The final blow occurred when halfway up the stairs the couch got stuck on the railings. *Really stuck.* The guys and I lost our patience, exchanged blaming words, and stood on each side of the lodged couch, glowering at each other.

I had a lot to learn about influence.

The Privilege of Influence

After experiencing brokenness and persevering in our purpose, God blesses us with the privilege of spiritual influence. But contrary to my sixteen-year-old logic, *influence isn't about power and getting what we want. It's about servanthood and giving our best to others,* whatever our position in life.

This is another principle of Christ's kingdom that's difficult for our control-oriented culture to grasp. We're encouraged to scramble to the top, revel in the perks, and discount the "little people" below. Yet Christ said in his kingdom the first shall be last and the last shall be first.[1] He taught his followers to influence through humility.

Until recent years I had difficulty understanding this concept. I enlarged my territory and tried controlling everything within it—and I honestly believed this was influence, a type of "keeping my ducks in a row" for God. I also thought humility required being passive about opportunity, an approach I didn't like or want. But then an older woman graced my life and turned my ideas about influence and spirituality upside down. She has taught me through humility, and "passive" would never describe her.

I first "met" Win years ago when a coworker dropped a brochure on my desk and asked, "Is this your mother?" I knew it couldn't be and barely looked up from my work.

"Why do you ask?" I questioned.

"She has your last name." That got my attention. Not many people bear the name Couchman.

Looking back at me from the brochure was a woman about the age of my mother but not a relative, or at least not one I had met. *How could this be?* Every Couchman I'd heard of was at least distantly related to me. This mystery woman also shared my interests—writing and speaking—and planned to teach at a conference in a nearby Chicago suburb. I had to meet her. I called Win, set a dinner appointment at the conference, and we've been friends ever since.

Win has a large capacity for life and doesn't miss one moment of it. After raising four children and enjoying years of church activities, she now devotes more time to writing, speaking, and teaching Bible studies. Win and her husband, Bob, defined retirement as traveling overseas to nurture missionaries with her teaching gift and his mechanical ability. Then when health problems stopped their global jaunts, they returned home to Wisconsin but didn't drop out. A continual stream of people still solicit Win's counsel, invite her to speak, or just keep in touch.

Win's involvements impress me, but she's influenced me the most with who she is. Through hardship and accomplishment she's earned the right to be revered, but Win doesn't take herself too seriously, and she openly confesses her failings. Though she's fairly well known to the public and an effective leader, Win practices a servanthood that profoundly affects women in her path. When she casually enters a room, younger women gravitate toward her to soak in her warmth and contemporary but sensible approach to life. And to laugh. With Winifred there's usually laughter.

A few years ago I asked Win to join a prayer team to intercede for projects I work on. She said yes without hesitation and began praying regularly for me and my requests. Occasionally she sends me notes and faxes, sympathizing when I'm discouraged and rejoicing when I'm encouraged. More than once she's said, "I'm committed to serving you. It's a privilege."

I'm touched by Win's humility. In the world's scheme I should be serving her. She's older and wiser, more creative and accomplished than I am, yet Win honors me. Along with other friends and circumstances, she's transformed my definition of success. Instead of assessing friends and acquaintances by what they do and the money they acquire, I wonder if they're giving, forgiving, and playful. I admire people who are at peace with themselves and devote time to fattening their souls. I want to ask whether they know their purpose in life and if they're graciously pursuing it. Gradually I'm growing more concerned about character than power, and friends who've known me for years consider this nothing short of a miracle.

Maybe I'm finally comprehending what God has been telling me all along: the fruit of the Holy Spirit is more important than the fruit of my labor. Love, joy, peace, patience, kindness, goodness, faithfulness, gentleness, self-control.[2] These are the qualities to covet; these open the gateway to influencing others deeply. These are what please God.

I've a lot of uprooting and replanting before I consistently bear this fruit, but in the meantime, through observation and experimentation I've pinpointed three ways I can express these characteristics and spiritually influence others. These aren't behaviors I've mastered; they constitute long-term goals. So once again I'm up to my neck in unfamiliar territory—right where God wants me to be so I'll lean on him.

While pursuing my purpose, I'm interested in influencing others by risking vulnerability, questing for quality, and focusing on unity, for these actions and attitudes make us spiritually influential.

Risking Vulnerability

If personal style indicates who we are, then I'm schizophrenic.

For years my professional wardrobe has been marked by simple lines, quality fabrics, and basic black heels for most everything. I'm uncomfortable in traditionally feminine clothes of lace and ribbons, ruffles and gathers, or dangling necklaces and earrings. And pink and lavender are definitely out.

My home reflects a different style altogether. Here I'm part Laura Ashley, part Martha Stewart before she delved into minimalism. Flowers bloom everywhere: on the rugs, the china, the paintings, the wallpaper. Every rose bouquet I've received for the last five years sits, dried and still colorful, in a vase somewhere in the house. I unabashedly mix patterns, collect cherub figurines, pouf out valances, and throw cushy pillows on couches and chairs. Shades of rose, blue, green, peach, and yellow splash throughout the rooms.

People who've only known me in a professional context turn speechless when they enter my home. First, there's the feminine decor; then there's me in shorts and a T-shirt with a spade or spatula in hand. The contrast jolts them, and usually they say, "I can't believe this is your house!" or more directly, "I can't believe this is you."

Until recent years I couldn't believe it was me, either. How could I be one woman in the workplace and another at home? And why did I try so hard to keep the two separate?

I was afraid. And uncomfortable with myself.

I feared if men at work saw my feminine side, they'd stereotype me and thwart my forward movement. (I'd seen this happen to other women.) I feared if certain friends and neighbors detected my assertive and professional self, they'd reject me, too. I couldn't imagine anyone accepting the whole me, not even myself. As a result, I lived like a cardboard, two-sided woman, flipping sides to fit the situation.

I finally grew tired of the professional/personal dividing line and wanted to be the real me—the whole me—all of the time. As I became more secure in God's acceptance, I asked, "Why don't I be everything he created me to be, instead of who 'they' think I should be?" I wanted to integrate, and integration pivoted on truthfulness. With work associates I needed to drop my guard, strip the facade of having it all together, let them see the vulnerable me. In friendships I wanted to stop trying to please everybody and become more outspoken.

It all felt terrifying, but as I let out the real me bit by bit, I learned two surprising truths: all along I hadn't fooled anyone, and when I chose to be vulnerable, I earned people's trust. I'd spent so much time bucking up and being a professional, hoping to gain coworkers' admiration, yet what they respected was my willingness to sob openly. I'd devoted years to restraining myself in certain relationships, and these friends preferred my loud desperation about life.

The truth be told, most people want honesty, but candor is risky and messy. Some people, even some I've counted as friends, have used my vulnerability against me; they've clobbered me with my failings, leaving me emotionally bruised and bloodied. But like the Velveteen

Rabbit I am becoming Real, though some think of it as shabby. I want my hair loved off, my eyes dropped out, my joints loosened up. "But these things don't matter at all, because once you are Real you can't be ugly, except to people who don't understand."[3]

Besides, God understands and approves.

And most important, this is how we can be like Jesus.

Questing for Quality

When we needed something done around the house, my farm-grown parents usually fixed, constructed, or moved it themselves. I've carried this self-reliant mentality into my home, surviving sticky wallpaper falling on my head, spattering as much paint on myself as on the ceiling, and accidentally dropping furniture down the stairs so that it acquired a "weathered" look. From mishaps like these I've learned that outside of a computer keyboard or a Calphalon skillet, I'm not deft with my hands.

But my friend Mary is, so I hired her to paint the kitchen cabinets. For the last month she's worked evenings and weekends patiently cleaning, sanding, masking, undercoating, and applying several layers of white paint to dark, grimy wood. Her attention to detail astounds me. Mary has carefully numbered the cabinets and their removed handles and screws so she'll reinsert them correctly. (I would have thrown them into a pile.) She's painted several doors because they didn't meet her standards and brought her own supplies to fill in cracks and repair minor flaws. (I would have slopped right over the imperfections.)

Every night when she's finished, Mary carefully cleans the brushes, seals the paint cans, and neatly folds and stacks the plastic drop cloth and usable newspapers. (I would have left a mess.)

Mary cares about the quality of her work, and that quality indicates she cares about me. Observing her process, I think of the saying, "God is in the details." Attention to detail demands much patience and love applied to tedious and humble tasks. These qualities reflect the Master Creator. (Who, after all, keeps up with the sparrows?) This quest for quality, when applied to our purpose, touches hearts.

The Dutch art historian H. R. Rookmaker called this attention to detail, to quality, the essence of everyday life. "Each life is an individual possession, but each life also touches the lives of others, in community.... At every point we are involved with others, working in and for the world to renew and maintain it, to set things right, to restore peace. We are to do this not primarily on a large scale, but in a small way among the people around us, which is the most difficult thing of all!"4

Each time I visit Chicago I roam the city's formidable art institute. Within its massive walls all kinds of people of various ages view many styles of artwork. Huge masterpieces adorn spacious rooms, but the gallery that truly transfixes museum visitors displays art in miniature.

The Thorne Miniature Rooms depict highlights from American and European architecture, decorative arts, and interior design between 1600 and 1940. Sixty-eight lighted boxes transport visitors to the homes of common and wealthy people past, with superb precision and craftsmanship. A wood-inlaid table supports a hand-painted tea set.

A bouquet of flowers in a sculpted vase rests on a harpsichord's closed lid. A magnificent couch could sit in my hand, with plenty of room left over. Tiny chandeliers, clocks, and fireplaces gleam with detail, prompting visitors to ask, "How did they do that?"

A book about the Thorne Rooms warns, "It is important not to underestimate the appeal of the workmanship displayed in the Thorne Rooms. The detail in each room is invariably astonishing, the delicacy of execution exquisite."[5] Paging through the book and recalling the reverence I felt looking at those rooms, I wonder what would happen if we applied similar care and precision to a life purpose and those affected by it. I can't help but believe when we care about the details, the quality, on a small scale, we will influence people in big ways.

Focusing on Unity

A few blocks from my home an old barnyard sits on the edge of a business district, a stubborn survivor of the city's steady sprawl. I've wondered how many accidents this slice of country life causes as it sits (and smells) unexpectedly at a busy intersection between commercial and residential neighborhoods. But it's not the rural ambiance that dis-tracts motorists; it's the proverbs the owner paints on the side of an old barn facing the north and west traffic.

Twenty-three years ago the owner recovered from a life-threatening brain tumor and told her children, "I feel well enough for a party, and you can even paint the barn." So that's what the family did, and almost every year a new, thought-provoking quotation appears on the barn's backside. The current slogan proclaims, "What humanity is is you being you and me being me and no add ons."[6]

This proverb causes me to think about my expectations toward the people in my life and especially the women, because they're the recipients of my life purpose. Do I let them be themselves, with no add ons? Or do I expect them to be like me? Do I respect their purposes in life or that they may feel no destiny at all?

A candid answer would be "It depends."

I give a wide berth to my close circle of friends and family, allowing them choices, opinions, interests, and purposes divergent from mine. But enlarging the circumference of my relationships with Christians, let alone with non-Christians, betrays a different attitude. I sometimes become impatient and judgmental. I fail to understand certain women's choices and don't hesitate to say so, as if I'm the arbitrator of right and wrong.

If I examine these judgments, I find they're usually not based on other women's sin or indifference. (We should never abandon our concern about sin, but moral rebellion is not what I'm referring to here.) Their choices and life purposes are just dissimilar to mine.

I'm embarrassed to confess my selective judgments, but the admission will help me change. Contrary to my critical lapses, I want redeemed women of all ages and purposes to enjoy and learn from their differing choices and purposes. If we sincerely extend Christ's love to one another, even when we don't understand one another, we could profoundly influence the world. More important, God desires that we live in unity with the "different" woman next door or across an ocean.

During his ministry on earth, Jesus emphasized that his followers should love one another,[7] and kneeling in a garden before his arrest and crucifixion he prayed we would all be one.[8] I am amazed that facing the worst ordeal of his earth-bound life, Christ focused on asking the Father to keep the spiritual family together. Given our divisive natures, he recognized what a monumental task this would be.

The apologist Francis A. Schaeffer called this unity "the mark of a Christian." He explained: "We are to love all true Christian brothers [and sisters] in a way that the world may observe. This means showing love to our brothers in the midst of our differences—great and small—loving our brothers when it costs us something, loving them even under times of tremendous emotional tension, loving them in a way the world can see.... Love—and the unity it attests to—is the mark Christ gave Christians to *wear* before the world. Only with this mark may the world know that Christians are indeed Christians and that Jesus was sent by the Father."[9]

One way we express this love is by celebrating our diverse life purposes and God-inspired visions, as well as the personal choices that flow from them. This celebration is easier to describe than practice. For example, the mommy wars, still hot after years of aggravation, divide spiritual sisters along ragged lines. Both mothers who work in the marketplace and mothers who stay home with children feel criticized for their child-rearing decisions. Free-floating hurt and anger fester between them, so much so that to manage certain relationships I avoid discussing the topic altogether.

But what if Christian women could drop their grievances and respect one another's opinions, recognizing that each mother needs to hear from God, and he may give us different answers? What if, instead of fighting we began truly listening to and supporting one another, regardless of our parenting decisions?

The marketplace is another example where spiritual women could make a remarkable difference. Whether it's a secular business or a Christian organization, the workplace fills with gossip and divisiveness. Too many of us know it as a place we can't trust other women, for fear they'll smear our reputation, undermine our work, or edge us out of deserved recognition. This can also describe churches, neighborhoods, and community groups—any place we rub elbows, trying to express our distinctiveness.

But what if the Christian women in these places forsook jealousy, competitiveness, and being judgmental to humbly embrace, learn from, and serve one another in love? What if we celebrated our diverse life purposes instead of drawing comparisons that always bring somebody up short?

If we did any one of these things, we'd become a powerful spiritual force.

An accomplished sculptor once worked feverishly on a new piece of art, yet toiled in private so none of his students could observe the emerging masterpiece.

Finally one day he unveiled the magnificent sculpture of a woman to a protégé.

The student gasped at the beauty. After inspecting the entire work, he exclaimed, "It's marvelous! But those hands—they are exquisite! So well sculpted, so lifelike, so detailed. Ah, those hands!"

The teacher's face filled with disgust. He picked up a hammer and smashed the hands, then blow by blow he destroyed the entire sculpture. Turning to the shocked young man, he raged, "No, no, no! The hands must not stand out! They should not be more important than any other part of the work. Each part of the body should contribute equally to the whole."

So what's to stop us from designing a purposeful life and together influencing the world with the beautiful aroma of God?

We hold the answer not in our hands but in our hearts.

Celebration

Joining Hands for the Journey

☙

The waves echo behind me....
But there are other beaches to explore.
There are more shells to find.
This is only a beginning.

ANNE MORROW LINDBERGH

MELISSA CALLED early this morning, plucking me from slumber. As I pushed into consciousness, I heard my niece describe a summer job, an on-again, off-again romance, life with roommates, and her impending college graduation. The conversation reminds me that four years have passed since we celebrated the end of her high school days—and that we grow older quickly.

Soon we will plan another celebration, bringing closure to her college ambitions and opening wide the working world. Again, as that night in a French restaurant, I draw comparisons between us, but this time similarities instead of differences cause me to reflect. Without my prompting, Melissa enrolled in the same university, the same journalism department as I did more than twenty years ago. We swap stories and laugh about learning from a kooky professor, soaking up an intense photography course, fighting for space in the school's parking lots, and enduring boring summer classes.

Hearing the tiredness in Melissa's voice and thinking of my past failures due to overscheduling, I repress the urge to lecture her about slowing down. Not unlike the younger me, Melissa collects activities as though they're medallions that can't be won later if she refuses them now. In letters to me her mother, older sister, and grandmother casually comment that "Melissa is so busy we rarely see her anymore." I worry about her burning out but realize I am assessing her college-age capacity by my fortysomething energy level.

Although she always politely listens to my opinions, I must resist trying to clone myself through Melissa (a goal she would not allow anyway) and remember to manage our generation gap respectfully. Though our interests and backgrounds intertwine, she is distinctly herself. Melissa must find her own way, her own divinely inspired vision, as she journeys toward purpose. I can love, advise, and encourage, but she will form decisions and make mistakes bearing her indelible imprint. I cannot load my expectations on this niece, orchestrating the turns of her life. That job belongs to God.

Instead I will welcome her into another stage of womanhood,

offering the best advice I know: *All your life be faithful to your purpose, to whom the Creator designed you to be.*

These are wise words for every woman, for they originate with God. And with these words I'll remind Melissa that none of us travels alone. On every side we're flanked by spiritual sisters who'll assist and encourage if we but reach out a hand. Individually yet together we pursue purpose and make a difference in the world.

This is my hope for her.

This is what makes a life worth living.

Notes

Chapter One: Significance

1. Ecclesiastes 1:2.

2. Carl L. Becker, *Progress and Power* (Stanford, Calif.: Stanford University Press, 1936), 101.

3. Isaiah 40:11.

4. Psalm 8:3—5.

5. Deuteronomy 32:10; Psalm 17:8.

6. Psalm 22:9—10; 71:6; 139:13; Isaiah 44:2.

7. Mother Teresa and Brother Roger, *Seeking the Heart of God: Reflections on Prayer* (San Francisco: HarperCollins Publishers, 1991), 20—21.

8. Isaiah 49:15.

9. The poem "The Hound of Heaven" by Francis Thompson (1859—1907) describes the author's futile flight from God, who relentlessly pursues him.

10. Jeremiah 31:3.

11. Thomas Merton, *The New Man* (Toronto: Bantam Books, 1961), 6.

12. James and Marti Hefley, *By Their Blood* (Grand Rapids: Baker Book House, 1979), 43.

13. Matthew 16:26.

Chapter Two: Purpose

1. Lauralee Mannes, "Welcome to Sister Gena's Place," *Clarity*, May/June 1994. Used by permission.

2. 1 Timothy 2:2.

3. Matthew 19:26.

4. *Webster's New World Dictionary*, 2d college ed., s.v. "purpose."

5. Richard Nelson Bolles, *How to Find Your Mission in Life* (Berkeley: Ten Speed Press, 1991), 12—24.

6. The Presbyterian Church in America, *The Confession of Faith*, 2d ed. (Atlanta: Committee for Christian Education and Publications, 1986).

7. Deuteronomy 6:5; 13:3; Matthew 6:33.

8. Gelsey Kirkland with Greg Lawrence, *Dancing on My Grave* (Garden City, New York: Doubleday and Company, Inc., 1986), 76—77.

9. Deuteronomy 10:12—13.

10. Corrie Ten Boom, *Not Good If Detached* (Fort Washington, Pa.: Christian Literature Crusade, 1957), 18.

11. Ibid., 19—20.

12. Exodus 33:17; Matthew 10:30.

13. 1 Corinthians 6:20; Galatians 3:26—29.

14. Psalm 139:13—16 The Message.

15. 1 Corinthians 12:12—26.

16. 1 Corinthians 12:4—6.

Chapter Three: Authenticity

1. 1 Kings 19:11—12.

2. 2 Timothy 1:7.

3. James 4:7.

4. Catherine Marshall, *The Helper* (Lincoln, Va.: Chosen Books, 1978), 35.

5. Hannah Whitall Smith, *Daily Devotions from The Christian's Secret of a Happy Life* (Old Tappan, N. J.: Fleming H. Revell Company, 1984), 87.

6. A. W. Tozer, *Man the Dwelling Place of God* (Harrisburg, Pa.: Christian Publications, Inc., 1966), 40.

7. Catherine Marshall, *Light in My Darkest Night* (Carmel, N. Y.: Guideposts, 1989), 210.

8. Marsha Sinetar, *Do What You Love, the Money Will Follow* (New York: Dell, 1987), 73—74.

9. Quotation credited to J. Stone.

10. John 10:10; 8:32.

11. *Chariots of Fire,* prod. David Puttnam, 124 min., Warner Home Video, 1982, videocassette.

12. Matthew 25:14—29; Luke 19:12—27.

13. For a listing and explanation of spiritual gifts, see 1 Corinthians 12—14.

14. Bolles, *Find Your Mission,* 43.

15. Psalm 37:4.

16. Frederick Buechner, *Wishful Thinking: A Theological ABC* (New York: Harper and Row, Publishers, 1973), 95.

17. Marsha Sinetar, *To Build the Life You Want, Create the Work You Love* (New York: St. Martin's Press, 1995), 47.

18. H. G. Spafford and P. P. Bliss, "It Is Well with My Soul" in *Hymns of the Christian Life* (Harrisburg, Pa.: Christian Publications, Inc., 1936), 125.

19. Psalm 90:17.

20. Psalm 37:23—24 The Amplified Bible.

Chapter Four: Vision

1. Puck appears in *A Midsummer Night's Dream,* in *Shakespeare: The Complete Works,* ed. G. B. Harrison (New York: Harcourt, Brace and World, Inc., 1968), 520.

2. John Bartlett, *Familiar Quotations* (Boston: Little, Brown and Company, 1980), 322.

3. Proverbs 29:18 King James Version.

4. Abraham H. Maslow, *Motivation and Personality,* 3d ed. (New York: Harper and Row, Publishers, Inc., 1987), 15–22.

5. Carly Simon, "The Stuff that Dreams Are Made Of" on *Coming Around Again,* Arista, audiocassette.

6. Calvin Miller, *The Singer* (Downers Grove, Ill.: InterVarsity Press, 1975), 81.

7. Psalm 81:10; Romans 15:13; Isaiah 29:8 KJV.

8. Ephesians 3:16–21.

9. Deuteronomy 4:24; Hebrews 12:29.

10. Madeleine L'Engle, *Walking on Water: Reflections on Faith and Art* (Wheaton, Ill.: Harold Shaw Publishers, 1980), 67.

11. Ezekiel 1; Luke 1:26–38; Acts 9:1–22.

12. Isaiah 52:7.

13. Isobel Kuhn, *By Searching* (Chicago: Moody Press, 1959), 4, 160.

14. Matthew 19:30; James 4:6; 1 Peter 5:5.

15. Colossians 3:23.

16. Frank Schaeffer, *Portofino* (New York: Macmillan Publishing Co., Inc., 1992), 246.

17. Habakkuk 2:3.

Chapter Five: Focus

1. Ralph G. Martin, *Henry and Clare: An Intimate Portrait of the Luces* (New York: G. P. Putnam's Sons, 1991), 408.

2. Ann Spangler, ed., *Bright Legacy: Portraits of Ten Outstanding Christian Women* (Ann Arbor, Mich.: Servant Books, 1983), 124–49.

3. *Webster's New World Dictionary*, s.v. "focus."

4. Laurie Lisle, *Portrait of an Artist: A Biography of Georgia O'Keeffe* (New York: Washington Square Press, 1980), 103.

5. Anne Wilson Schaef, *Meditations for Women Who Do Too Much* (San Francisco: HarperSanFrancisco, 1990), March 29 entry.

6. Craig Nakken, *The Addictive Personality: Roots, Rituals, and Recovery* (Minneapolis: Hazelden, 1988), 21–23.

7. 2 Corinthians 5:7.

8. Hebrews 12:1–2 KJV.

9. Romans 8:28.

10. Ecclesiastes 3:1–8.

Chapter Six: Brokenness

1. John 16:33.

2. Isaiah 61:3.

3. Chaim Potok, *The Chosen* (New York: Fawcett Crest, 1967), 260–68.

4. Ibid., 267.

5. Isaiah 42:3.

6. Philippians 2:17.

7. T. Alton Bryant, ed., *The New Compact Bible Dictionary* (Grand Rapids: Zondervan Publishing House, 1967), 139, 419.

8. 2 Timothy 4:6–7.

9. Karen Burton Mains, *With My Whole Heart: Disciplines for Strengthening the Inner Life* (Portland, Ore.: Multnomah Press, 1987), 144.

10. Exodus 34:6–7.

11. Lamentations 3:22–23.

12. Book of Jonah.

13. Romans 2:4.

14. Acts 5:1–10.

15. Psalm 66:17–18.

16. 1 Peter 3:13–14a, 15–17.

17. "Key Lessons from the Sermon on the Mount," in Life Application Bible, New International Version (Wheaton, Ill. and Grand Rapids, Mich.: Tyndale House Publishers and Zondervan Publishing House, 1991), 1653.

18. 2 Corinthians 12:7–10.

19. Hannah Hurnard, *Hinds' Feet on High Places* (Wheaton, Ill.: Tyndale House Publishers, Inc., 1977), 241.

20. Isaiah 53:3–5, author's italics.

21. Hebrews 12:11, author's italics.

Chapter Seven: Perseverance

1. Ana Gascón Ivey, "Down in the Dumps in Guatemala," *Clarity*, July/August 1994. Used by permission.

2. Deuteronomy 23:23.

3. Paul Tournier, *Reflections: A Personal Guide for Life's Most Crucial Questions* (Philadelphia: The Westminster Press, 1976), 130.

4. Psalm 25:6; 52:8; 100:5; 111:3; 119:152, 160; 135:13; 136:1; 138:8; 1 Peter 1:25.

5. 1 Samuel 15:22.

6. Martha Thatcher, *The Freedom of Obedience: Choosing the Way of True Liberation* (Colorado Springs: NavPress, 1986), 110.

7. Joshua 4:6–7 New American Standard Version.

8. Mark 5:15.

9. 1 Peter 5:8.

10. Mark I. Bubeck, *The Adversary: The Christian Versus Demon Activity* (Chicago: Moody Press, 1975), 79.

11. Ephesians 6:13–17.

12. Hebrews 11:13–16.

13. Genesis 22:1–18.

14. Laurie Beth Jones, *Jesus, CEO: Using Ancient Wisdom for Visionary Leadership* (New York: Hyperion, 1994), 157–58.

Chapter Eight: Influence

1. Matthew 19:30.

2. Galatians 5:22–23.

3. Margery Williams, *The Velveteen Rabbit: Or How Toys Become Real* (New York: Avon Books, 1975), 17.

4. H. R. Rookmaker, *The Creative Gift* (Westchester, Ill.: Cornerstone Books, 1981), 68–69.

5. Bruce Hatton Boyer, "Creating the Thorne Rooms," in *Miniature Rooms: The Thorne Rooms at the Art Institute of Chicago* (New York and Chicago: Abbeville Press and The Art Institute of Chicago, 1983), 9.

6. "Twenty-three years of barnyard wisdom," *Colorado Springs Gazette Telegraph,* 6 July.

7. John 13:34.

8. John 17:11, 22–23.

9. Francis A. Schaeffer, *The Church at the End of the 20th Century* (Downers Grove, Ill.: InterVarsity Press, 1970), 152–53.

Exploration

Questions for Groups or Individuals

*Learning what's going on inside you can be difficult,
but it's also invigorating, and the rewards are enormous.
You can do anything if you only know what it is.
And you're about to find out.*

BARBARA SHER

AFTER READING each chapter, you can use these questions to clarify your feelings and response to it.

Chapter One: Significance

1. Look up the Scriptures listed in these chapter one footnotes: 3–6, 8, 10. How do they speak to you about your significance to God?

2. What might keep you from embracing your deep significance to God?

3. How could embracing this significance change your life and attitudes?

Chapter Two: Purpose

1. On a scale of 1 (poor) to 10 (excellent), what's your score for fulfilling the first purpose of living in God's presence? How about the second purpose of making the world a better place? Explain your scores.

2. Consider your third purpose: exercising your greatest talent for God's work in the world. How could your purpose express your uniqueness?

3. What could keep you from pursuing each of the three purposes? Why?

Chapter Three: Authenticity

1. What are your talents and spiritual gifts? What are your dreams? What is your calling?

2. When forming your purpose, how can you stay true to the woman within?

3. What could be your purpose in life? Write a rough draft of a mission statement.

Chapter Four: Vision

1. Describe one vision related to your purpose. Why is this vision important to you?

2. What barriers might you need to overcome to fulfill this vision? How could you overcome them?

3. How can you cultivate "a new way of seeing" that believes in your vision?

Chapter Five: Focus

1. To pursue your vision, how will you need to focus your life? What changes will this entail?

2. In regard to your focus, how might God ask you to risk? How do you feel about this?

3. What responsibilities do you need to weigh against your focus? What are their priorities compared to your focus?

Chapter Six: Brokenness

1. How have you felt broken in your life? How might this brokenness contribute to your purpose?

2. How might sin be hindering the effectiveness of your purpose?

3. What personal weakness affects your purpose? How could God use it as a strength?

Chapter Seven: Perseverance

1. What are the specific biblical reasons you should persevere with your purpose?

2. What memorials could you build to God's past faithfulness? How could these memorials encourage you?

3. How can you prepare for spiritual warfare?

Chapter Eight: Influence

1. How would you like to influence the world?
2. In the past what have you misunderstood about influence?
3. How will (do) you know you're influencing others through your purpose?

Discovery

More Books about Purposeful Living

The most pathetic person in the world
is someone who has sight but has no vision.

HELEN KELLER

ALTHOUGH NOT ALL of these books support a Christian viewpoint, they present truths about the topics in *Designing a Woman's Life*. Read with discernment, these titles can enhance the search for purpose.

Bolles, Richard Nelson. *How to Find Your Mission in Life*. Berkeley: Ten Speed Press, 1991.

Covey, Stephen R. *The Seven Habits of Highly Effective People*. New York: Simon and Schuster, 1989.

Friesen, Gary and J. Robin Maxson. *Decision Making and the Will of God*. Sisters: Ore.: Multnomah, 1983.

Heald, Cynthia. *Becoming a Woman of Purpose.* Colorado Springs: NavPress, 1994.

McCarthy, Kevin W. *The On-Purpose Person.* Colorado Springs: Piñon Press, 1992.

Myers, Warren and Ruth. *Discovering God's Will.* Colorado Springs: NavPress, 1980.

Potter, Beverly. *Finding a Path with a Heart.* Berkeley: Ronin Publishing, 1995.

Sheehy, Gail. *New Passages.* New York: Random House, 1995.

Sher, Barbara. *I Could Do Anything If I Only Knew What It Was.* New York: Delacorte Press, 1994.

Sinetar, Marsha. *Do What You Love, the Money Will Follow.* New York: Dell Publishing, 1987.

Sinetar, Marsha. *To Build the Life You Want, Create the Work You Love.* New York: St. Martin's Press, 1995.

Stephan, Naomi. *Fulfill Your Soul's Purpose.* Walpole, N. H.: Stillpoint Publishing, 1994.

Stoddard, Alexandra. *Making Choices.* New York: Avon Books, 1994.

Tieger, Paul D. and Barbara Barron-Tieger. *Do What You Are.* Boston: Little, Brown and Company, 1992.

Trent, John. *Lifemapping.* Colorado Springs: Focus on the Family Publishing, 1994.

Viscott, David. *Risking.* New York: Pocket Books, 1977.